CHOCOLATE

For Mum, who is my inspiration.

CHOCOLATE

Luscious recipes and expert know-how
for biscuits, cakes, sweet treats & desserts

KIRSTEN TIBBALLS

MURDOCH BOOKS
SYDNEY · LONDON

We live in this incredible food world now. Food is on everybody's mind. Everyone is a cook in some way, shape or form. The credit goes to many people but, for me, the credit should go to the true chefs that have worked tirelessly day in, day out learning their craft. They love food, they are technique driven and are always striving for better, better and better. Why? Because they are obsessed by food and its craft. A true example of this is Kirsten. A pastry chef of the highest order, an extraordinary chocolatier and a wonderful teacher. I am so envious (in a positive way) of this wonderful lady's talents. Her commitment, drive, care and love for all things pastry is palpable. It's no wonder why her handmade chocolates were awarded best in the world.

To be a great pastry chef you need an impeccable sense of balance, the ability to go out on a limb, and to dream big. This is Kirsten, but more than that, she is a beautiful human, lovely lady and incredible person.

Envious I will always be.

— GEORGE CALOMBARIS

CONTENTS

INTRODUCTION

As a child, my mum would make sweet treats a few times a week from recipes passed down from her mother, such as steamed puddings, golden syrup dumplings, Scottish shortbread and many other personal favourites from her childhood. From a young age I discovered the joy that food can bring. Cooking with my mum was always a weekend activity that we looked forward to.

At fifteen years of age I started my apprenticeship at a small patisserie in Mornington, Victoria. My parents were fully supportive of me starting full-time work so young, as it had been a long-time dream of mine to become a pastry chef. I would start work at 2 am and finish when the job was done. My dad was tasked with driving me to the patisserie, leaving home at 1 am, five days a week, for the 50-minute drive to drop me at work before heading back home to grab a couple of hours sleep before getting up again for work himself. Mum would pick me up after she finished work at the end of my workday, which could be any time between 5 pm and 10 pm. She would patiently wait for me to call, unable to go out in case I finished work late (of course, there were no mobile phones at this time), and would often come into the patisserie to help me wash dishes and clean the floor so I could get an extra hour of sleep. My parents did this for three years until I was old enough to get my driver's licence. Their unwavering support and commitment to me is the reason I am as successful as I am today. The intensive work hours, often up to 20 hours a day, fast-tracked my skills and gave me a great start as a qualified pastry chef.

I love what I do and I love instilling my passion in others and watching them develop their own skills and abilities. This is why I opened Savour Chocolate & Patisserie School in 2002; to share what I know and love with people from all over the world.

I chose chocolate as the main theme for this book for its diversity and my love of it, from the cocoa bean through to a finished brownie. I travel the world demonstrating and teaching new and innovative techniques to other professionals, but it is often the simple products that are the most enjoyable. This book contains a variety of really simple recipes through to more complex ones. But the complex recipes can be broken down into simpler components – and not every element has to be made on the same day.

Chocolate is hard enough to resist in its purest form, and even harder when you add more sugar and cream! If we are going to indulge in sneaky guilty pleasures, why not make them sensational? That's my philosophy behind this book. If you're going to put in the effort to make one of my recipes I will make sure it is worth your while by giving you a deliciously decadent chocolate experience that you may find difficult to share.

I hope you love making – and sharing – my favourite chocolate recipes.

NOTES ON THE RECIPES

Creating recipes at home should be easy and rewarding. You don't need expensive gadgets or hard-to-obtain ingredients to achieve incredible food. Delicious desserts and cakes are best made with simple ingredients. I confess I'm a little fussy about particular ingredients, but these can make a world of difference to the end flavour and texture. Here are a few tips about how to select and use ingredients to get the most scrumptious results from your chocolate creations, as well as a few explanations of terms you will see in this book. For information about some key kitchen tools used in this book, have a look at the equipment notes on page 250.

Butter: I generally use unsalted butter in my recipes, which gives me the ability to control how much salt I'm adding. It's easier to work with the butter if it is chopped into cubes prior to adding it to a recipe.

Cocoa & Dutch-process cocoa powder: There are two types of unsweetened cocoa powder on the market: standard and Dutch process. I've only used Dutch-process cocoa powder for the recipes in this book. 'Dutch process' refers to the cocoa being alkaline treated, making it richer in flavour, darker in colour and more easily dissolvable than standard cocoa. There are various grades of Dutch-process cocoa powder, but look out for varieties with around 24% cocoa butter, which will help keep the baked goods delicious and moist.

Compound chocolate: I'm not a fan of compound chocolate, which is a cheaper alternative to couverture. Compound chocolate replaces naturally occurring cocoa butter with hydrogenated vegetable fats, often derived from palm oil. Unlike couverture, compound chocolate will melt and set without any tempering. However, as the vegetable fats in compound chocolate have a higher melting point than cocoa butter, it can leave a waxy film in your mouth and leave you disappointed in the taste. Always check the ingredients on the chocolate package to determine if you are purchasing compound chocolate – it will have vegetable fat listed.

Couverture chocolate: Couverture is a divine type of chocolate, which I try to purchase in small quantities so I'm not tempted to eat the leftovers! I use the Callebaut brand of couverture chocolate in my recipes, which I simply refer to as 'good-quality chocolate' throughout the book.

Couverture is made from cocoa beans – the beans extracted from cocoa pods – which are around 50% cocoa butter and 50% dry cocoa solids. The cocoa butter melts and dissipates at a low temperature, giving it a beautiful mouthfeel as well as giving shine, gloss and snap to chocolate. Dry cocoa solids carry all the flavour.

Chocolate will often display the percentage of cocoa on the packaging. This percentage is a combination of both cocoa butter and dry cocoa solids – most often it will have a higher percentage of cocoa butter than dry cocoa solids, with the remaining ingredients made up of sugar, and milk powder for milk chocolate. Always check the packaging to ensure it contains cocoa butter.

Couverture chocolate needs to be tempered if you're using it to create a garnish, but not when you're adding it to other ingredients, such as a cake batter. Don't be intimidated by tempering – as you'll see in the method outlined in the Techniques section on pages 12–14, it's a straightforward process.

Storing chocolate: Chocolate is best stored in opaque packaging and sealed at all times to avoid it absorbing moisture from the atmosphere. Ideally, chocolate should be stored at temperatures between 15°C and 23°C (59°F and 73°F).

If chocolate is stored next to aromatic ingredients it can take on those flavours. Buy smaller quantities of chocolate so you're not storing it for long periods and therefore keeping it fresher. Finally, if your household is full of chocolate lovers, like mine, take care to hide it away from hungry kids and partners!

Cream: I have used pouring cream in the recipes with a 35% fat content. You can also use a UHT, or long-life, cream which will extend the shelf life of the chocolates.

Cream of tartar: Cream of tartar is a natural product derived from grapes and sold in powdered form. When added to egg whites before whisking, the acidity in the cream of tartar will create a much creamier meringue.

Dacquoise: A dacquoise is a meringue sponge made with nuts and flour. It's deliciously crunchy on the outside and chewy in the centre.

Dry ingredients: Ensure that all dry ingredients are sifted prior to using them in a recipe.

Eggs: It's always better for eggs to be at room temperature when using them in a recipe. Room temperature egg whites will incorporate more air when whisked than refrigerated eggs. You'll also get better results when whisking older egg whites.

I have used 60 g (2 oz) eggs in this book. However, you'll note that amounts of whole eggs, egg whites and egg yolks are all given by weight – which is the most exact way of measuring ingredients.

When whisking egg whites, always ensure your bowl is clean as any fat residue left in the bowl will prevent them from fully whipping. To guarantee smooth and creamy whisked egg whites, always add a pinch of cream of tartar.

Flour: Flour comes in many varieties and strengths – the stronger the flour the more gluten it contains. We don't require a strong flour for any of the recipes you'll find in the book – a plain (all-purpose) flour is perfect.

Food colouring: There are generally three different types of food colourings available: water-based, oil-based, and gel. You should only use good-quality oil-based colours for chocolate work as water-based colours tend to stain chocolate, though they have other applications outside of chocolate work. Additionally, not all food colourings are bake stable, meaning they can change colour during the baking process. Look for bake-stable gel (for non-chocolate work) and oil-based colours, which are better for baking.

Ganache: A ganache is a mixture of liquid and chocolate that is emulsified to create a creamy soft texture.

Marzipan: Also known as almond paste, marzipan is a combination of almonds and sugar sold in solid form. The percentage on the package indicates the volume of nuts rather than sugar. I use a 50% almond paste.

Milk: I only use fresh, full-fat (whole) milk in the recipes, although it's also fine to use UHT, or long-life, milk.

Ovens: I've used a fan-forced oven for the recipes in this book. If you're using a conventional oven, set the temperature 20°C (68°F) higher than the temperature listed in the recipes.

Quenelle: A quenelle refers to an egg-shaped scoop of, generally, ice cream or cream. A quenelle can be created by dipping a dessertspoon into hot water, drying it, then scraping it along the surface of the ice cream or cream to create the distinctive egg-shaped curl.

Storage: The storage of your finished product is important so that you can ensure you're serving it in the best condition. Any of the products that are coated in chocolate are best stored at room temperature as long as your room temperature doesn't exceed 23°C (73°F). If the room temperature is warmer, seal the product in an airtight container and store it in the refrigerator.

Sugar: I prefer to use caster (superfine) sugar in recipes as it's faster to dissolve than standard granulated sugar. Icing (confectioners') sugar is finer again, but it's not suited to all the recipes as its fine texture doesn't have the ability to assist when aerating or caramelising. There are many varieties of sugar available, with varying degrees of sweetness, but throughout this book I only use caster sugar, icing sugar and liquid glucose. Glucose is less sweet than standard sugar and often helps to avoid sugar re-forming as a crystal once it has dissolved.

Tempering: This is the process that controls the way you heat and cool chocolate to achieve the ultimate snap, gloss and mouthfeel. For detailed instructions about tempering, see pages 12–14.

TECHNIQUES

Techniques are often simple tricks that can make a huge difference when cooking. I have included the techniques in this section that you will use over and over again when creating recipes from this book. You will find videos of these techniques on our YouTube channel (savourschool), or, for more in-depth instructions, you can subscribe to Savour Online classes via our website: savourschool.com.au. I am spoilt with my commercial kitchen, which has the space and equipment for pretty much any recipe, but there are always alternatives to kitchen equipment that will still ensure a beautiful finished product – and all the recipes in the book have been created for the domestic kitchen.

CHOCOLATE

Melting

Don't be intimidated by melting chocolate – it's a simple process. There are two main methods for melting chocolate: in a microwave; or in a double boiler or bain-marie. In either case, you should first finely chop the chocolate if you're not using chocolate buttons and keep the chocolate away from water or steam.

When melting chocolate in a microwave, use a plastic bowl as glass retains too much heat. Heat the chocolate on high heat in 30-second intervals, stirring well in between, until the chocolate is melted to the temperature or consistency you require.

If you don't have a microwave, you can melt your chocolate in a double boiler or bain-marie. Select a (non-plastic) bowl that fits tightly on top of a medium saucepan. Fill the saucepan midway with water and bring it to the boil. Either turn the heat off or turn it down low and place the bowl with chocolate in it on top. Stir the chocolate until it is melted to the temperature and consistency you require. If you are melting a large volume of chocolate, you may need to remove the bowl and reheat the water occasionally. Keep checking that you still have water in the saucepan.

In both methods, if your chocolate begins to set again, you can also reheat it with a hair dryer. Remember to always keep chocolate in a well-sealed packet or container so it doesn't absorb moisture, which will make it thick when melted.

Tempering

Tempering is an easy technique once you know the process. I recommend that you watch my tempering video on our YouTube channel (savourschool), which will give you easy-to-follow visual instructions that will assist you in perfecting this technique. Tempering can be challenging if you have a warm kitchen – so if it's warmer than 27°C (81°F), I recommend you leave it for another day. Remember: lots of stirring, avoid glass bowls, and always test that your chocolate is tempered before using it.

Although there any many different methods for tempering chocolate, I've outlined three techniques: the first two are known as 'seeding'; the third as 'tabling'. In all cases, don't rely solely on a thermometer to tell you that your chocolate is tempered – always test the chocolate as outlined in the following instructions.

The first process is what I call the 50/50 method. Using the instructions in the previous section on melting, melt the chocolate until it is approximately 50% liquid and 50% solid chocolate. Remove it from the heat or microwave, and stir vigorously until all the solid chocolate is melted. After 5 minutes, if you still have solid lumps of chocolate, gently warm it up with a hair dryer to melt.

The second method of tempering is just as easy. Take the volume of chocolate you're using and set aside 25% in a separate bowl. Melt the other 75% of chocolate using the instructions in the previous section on melting and heat it to 45°C (113°F). Remove it from the heat or microwave, add the remaining 25% of chocolate and vigorously stir through until all melted. If necessary, lightly heat the chocolate with a hair dryer to melt any remaining solids after 5 minutes.

1. For the second method of tempering, add 25% of chocolate to the 75% of chocolate at 45°C (113°F).

2. Stir the chocolate through.

3. If all the chocolate hasn't melted after 5 minutes, use a hair dryer to gently heat it.

The third method for tempering chocolate is tabling. This method will give you the same end result as the previous two, although it's considered to give a more consistent finish. You'll need a stone surface for this technique – stone is always cooler than the room temperature so it helps to cool the chocolate down quickly. Melt the chocolate to 45°C (113°F) then pour two-thirds onto the stone surface and mix it on the

1. To temper using the tabling method, mix two-thirds of the melted chocolate on a stone surface with a scraper.

2. Scrape the chocolate back to the centre of the bench and out again until the temperature reduces to 27°C (81°F).

3. Scrape the chocolate back into a bowl and combine with the remaining one-third of unmelted chocolate. Stir vigorously.

work surface with a metal scraper. Scrape the chocolate back into the centre of the work surface, to allow the work surface to cool the chocolate down, and then scrape it out again. Repeat this process until the chocolate cools to 27°C (81°F). You will notice the chocolate thickening slightly when it reaches this temperature. Scrape it back into the original bowl with the remaining one-third of chocolate and stir vigorously. Do a test before using the chocolate to ensure that it is tempered.

For all tempering methods, use a thermometer to check the temperature of the liquid chocolate. The correct temperature for tempered dark chocolate is 31–32°C (88–90°F); 30–31°C (86–88°F) for milk chocolate; and 29–30°C (84–86°F) for white chocolate.

However, the temperature of the chocolate in a liquid state is not enough to determine if it's tempered. For the best evidence, take a small strip of baking paper and dip it into the chocolate, tap off the excess to ensure you have a thin layer and let it set at room temperature. Dark chocolate takes 5 minutes, milk chocolate 7 minutes and white chocolate 10 minutes to set at room temperature.

If the chocolate doesn't set within the time frame outlined above, it hasn't tempered. If the chocolate sets but it is streaky, it means the mixture needs more stirring and is very close to being tempered.

If, while you're working, your tempered chocolate starts to set, simply reheat it with a hair dryer before it sets too much and do another test.

Dipping

This technique is easy to achieve at home by simply replacing the more traditional dipping fork with a standard fork and using a skewer to stabilise the product while dipping.

For dipping, first line a tray with baking paper. You will require a dipping fork or standard fork and a few sheets of paper towel. Place one product at a time into the tempered chocolate and cover the top with a thin layer of chocolate. Pick up the product so that it sits half off your fork. Tap the fork a few times on the surface of the chocolate to remove any excess chocolate. Wipe the base of the fork on the side of the bowl and place the dipped product onto your prepared tray. Every 3–4 times you use the fork gently wipe it with some paper towel to avoid a build-up of chocolate. This technique is easiest if you use a small, deep bowl, so you have more depth with the chocolate.

I. *For dipping, press the chocolate bar into the milk chocolate.*

2. *Pull it out with a dipping fork and remove the excess chocolate from the base.*

3. *Place the dipped chocolate bars onto a lined tray.*

Making a ganache

A ganache is a mixture of liquid and chocolate. For example, it can be cream, fruit juice, water or milk combined with chocolate. The faster you combine the ingredients, the smoother the ganache will be. For a smooth and creamy result, I use a hand-held blender or a hand whisk.

Glazing

All the glazes in this book can be frozen for up to 4 weeks in a sealed container or kept for up to 4 days in the refrigerator. We usually use the glaze just below body heat, between 30–35°C (86–95°F). Reheat the glaze if necessary over low heat in a saucepan or in the microwave. If you find the glaze is too thick when reheating it, add a little water to adjust the viscosity. Always glaze a product when it's frozen for a clean finish.

1. *For the best finish, gently pour the glaze over already frozen products.*

2. *Use a palette knife to level the glaze on top of cakes.*

MOUSSES

Mixing

To create a light and creamy mousse, here are some helpful tips.

It's important when making a mousse that the chocolate is as warm as possible without over-heating it, particularly when it comes into contact with cold cream. We usually add the cream last in mousses and gently fold it through to ensure we maintain as much air as possible to keep the mousse light. Do not over-mix the mousse. Mix only until all the ingredients are combined then stop. If you do over-mix, the cream will separate and become grainy and you will lose all the aeration.

Freezing and unmoulding

Freezing is a great way to store a mousse cake before glazing and decorating it, and it makes it easy to handle.

Only when we create a mousse cake in a ring do we need to freeze it. Freezing the mousse cake is not detrimental to the quality, but enables you to remove the cake ring easily. If glazing a mousse cake, it must always be frozen first. To unmould a mousse cake it must be frozen to maintain straight and clean edges. The mousse cake should simply come out when gently pushed from the base. If you have not lined the side of the cake ring you will have to warm it to remove the ring. Once the ring is removed, store the cake in the freezer until you are ready to finish it.

CREAM

Whipping

Always ensure you use cold cream for whipping. If your kitchen is warm you should also chill the mixing bowl before whipping the cream. I use fresh cream with a 35% fat content. If you use a cream with a higher fat percentage the cream will be more difficult to whip, as it won't incorporate as much air into the mixture.

Semi-whipping

To semi-whip cream, whip just until the cream has some body but still collapses. Set the cream aside in the refrigerator until needed. It can be whipped up to an hour in advance.

BAKING

Preparing a cake ring

I prefer to use cake rings rather than tins, which means that you don't need to tip a cake upside-down to remove it. You can, of course, use a cake tin for any of the recipes in the book.

To line a cake ring, draw the base on baking paper by tracing around the circumference of the cake ring – this is called the base line. Add another 3 cm (1¼ inches) to the base line so that the baking paper is larger than your cake ring and cut. Make small incisions with scissors back to the base line about 2 cm (¾ inch) apart.

Spray the cake ring with some oil spray and ensure it sits on a flat tray lined with a baking mat or baking paper. Place the prepared baking paper base into the bottom of the cake ring so the fluted edges go up the side. Place a strip of baking paper slightly higher than the cake ring around the inside of the ring.

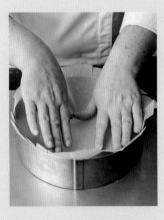

1. To prepare a cake ring press the baking paper base into the base of a greased ring or tin.

2. Line up the base, so the cut edge sits on the side of the ring or tin.

3. Place a strip of baking paper around the inside edge.

SHORTCRUST PASTRY

Making

When making shortcrust pastry we want the texture to be crumbly and buttery to eat – and I find it's best to use butter directly from the refrigerator.

There are two main methods for producing shortcrust pastry. The first is to rub the flour and butter together so the butter coats the flour particles and helps stop them from joining together and developing the gluten in the flour. The second method is to combine the butter and sugar together and then add the remaining ingredients, adding the flour last, and mixing only until the dough comes together.

It's important when making shortcrust pastry to not over-mix it. If it is over-mixed at any stage the gluten will start to develop and make the pastry more elastic and likely to shrink. It can also make the pastry tougher to eat.

With pie pastry we do develop the gluten, which means we must rest the pastry well, before rolling, to ensure the pastry doesn't shrink when rolling or during baking.

All the shortbread bases in the tart chapter, with the exception of the pie pastry, can be made on their own as a biscuit. This is always a great use of leftover pastry.

Rolling

Before you commence rolling, ensure that your pastry is firm and well rested. If you are making a large quantity of tarts, only roll out half the pastry at a time and place the remaining pastry in the refrigerator until required. Take any off-cuts left over from rolling out your first batch of tarts and add to the remaining pastry in the refrigerator. Then press the pastry together before rolling it again. This will ensure you don't overwork the pastry and develop the gluten.

Lightly dust the work surface with flour and place the pastry directly on top. Lightly dust the top surface of the pastry. Begin rolling out without applying too much pressure. After every roll, slide the pastry to the side and re-dust the bench to ensure the pastry doesn't stick. If the pastry starts cracking when you are rolling, it may be too cold and need to sit at room temperature for a few minutes before trying again. Continue dusting flour as you roll your pastry to the desired thickness. If it becomes too soft at any stage, just place it in the refrigerator again until it becomes firm. Alternatively, you can roll the pastry out between two sheets of baking paper, which will prevent it sticking to the work surface.

1. One method for making shortcrust pastry is to first rub the flour and butter together with your fingers.

2. Ensure your pastry is firm and well rested before rolling out.

3. Cut the rolled pastry slightly larger than the tart ring.

Lining a tart shell

I generally use plain tart rings for my tarts but you can also use fluted tart rings (preferably with the base removed). For individual tarts you can use egg rings if you don't have tart rings.

Have your tart rings ready on a tray so that as soon as the pastry is rolled it can be placed directly into the tart ring without warming up on the work surface.

Cut the rolled pastry slightly larger than the tart ring ensuring you have enough pastry to go up the sides with a little left over. Use a bowl or another object of a suitable diameter to use as a guide to trace around and cut your pastry. Gently pick your pastry up and centre it over the tart ring. Ensure the pastry is pressed and tucked right into the edge to avoid the pastry dropping and sliding while baking. Once you have pressed the pastry evenly into the tart ring place it in the refrigerator before trimming the top edge. Once the pastry firms up again, trim the edge with a small knife. Chilling the pastry before cutting it will give you a neat edge.

1. Gently press the pastry evenly to fit into the tart ring.

2. To blind bake, cover the pastry with baking paper and fill with uncooked rice.

3. Once the pastry has been blind baked, seal it with an egg yolk and milk mixture.

Blind baking

The reason we blind bake tarts is to ensure that the sides stay up during the baking process. As well, if you are making a tart with a baked liquid filling, sometimes the pastry doesn't cook right through to the base unless it is pre-cooked by blind baking.

To blind bake a tart, line the tart ring as described previously, then screw up some baking paper to soften it and cut it large enough to line the base and side of your tart shell. Place the softened paper into the un-baked tart case and gently press it to the edge. Fill the tart with uncooked rice – you can also use dried beans or baking beads. Press the rice into the tart shell so it fills the tart to the top.

Once you have prepared the tart, place it into a preheated oven and bake just until the sides will hold up once the rice is removed. Remove the rice and either place the tart back into the oven to continue baking until the tart is fully baked or place a filling into the tart that requires baking and continue the baking process.

Sealing

When filling a baked tart shell with a moist filling, it is best to seal the pastry first. You can brush the tart shell with egg yolk and a splash of milk as it comes out of the oven lightly coating the pastry surface while it is still hot, or brush the baked pastry with tempered chocolate once the pastry is cool.

PIPING

Making a paper piping cone

Some of the recipes call for a paper piping (icing) cone, which is simple to create. First, take a length of baking paper 30 x 40 cm (12 x 16 inches), fold it in half lengthways and cut it along the centre to create two 30 x 20 cm (12 x 8 inch) rectangles.

Line the two pieces of baking paper up and fold the right bottom corner up to the top left corner. The two corners won't meet but will make a 90 degree angle, with each edge overlapping the other by approximately 5 cm (2 inches). Cut along the diagonal crease with a sharp knife.

With one triangle, hold the longest edge of the triangle away from yourself with the cut-off edge in your right hand. Roll the right-hand point over once into the centre of the triangle and secure it with your left thumb. Pull the left-hand point around the outside of the bag once and pull it towards yourself, rather than wrapping it around the point of the cone. Continue to pull towards yourself until the tip is completely closed.

Fold the three points at the top of the bag down inside the bag and crease it to secure the bag. You are now ready to fill the bag. When filling the bag, fill it no more than halfway then ensure the seam of the bag is in the middle. Fold the top of the bag away from the seam, by folding the two corners in first, then roll the top edge of the bag down. Snip off the corner of the bag and you're ready to pipe! (You'll find video instructions for this on our YouTube channel - savourschool.)

1.

BISCUITS
& COOKIES

CHOCOLATE PECAN BISCUITS

MAKES: 45 DIFFICULTY: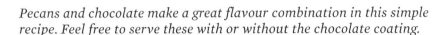

Pecans and chocolate make a great flavour combination in this simple recipe. Feel free to serve these with or without the chocolate coating.

125 g (4½ oz/1¼ cups) pecans
150 g (5½ oz) unsalted butter
150 g (5½ oz/⅔ cup) caster (superfine) sugar
1½ teaspoons ground cinnamon
90 g (3¼ oz/about 1½) whole eggs
125 g (4½ oz) good-quality dark chocolate, coarsely chopped
60 g (2¼ oz) self-raising flour
125 g (4½ oz) plain (all-purpose) flour, plus extra for dusting
½ teaspoon sea salt

CHOCOLATE PECAN BISCUITS

Preheat the oven to 160°C (315°F). Spread the pecans on a baking tray and roast them for 8–10 minutes. Once cool, roughly chop them.

Using an electric mixer with a paddle attachment, cream the butter and sugar on medium speed until light and creamy and the butter is fully incorporated – scrape the bowl down at regular intervals. Add the cinnamon and eggs.

Melt the dark chocolate in a double boiler or in a bowl in the microwave (see page 12). Add the chocolate to the butter mixture and continue to mix, scraping down the side of the bowl as needed, until combined. Finally add the dry ingredients and chopped pecans. Continue mixing just until combined and a dough forms. Press the dough into an even, flat square, wrap it in plastic wrap and place it in the refrigerator to rest for 1 hour, until firm.

Preheat the oven to 170°C (325°F) and line a baking tray with a non-stick mat or baking paper. Remove the dough from the refrigerator and let it sit at room temperature for a few minutes before rolling it out. Lightly dust a work surface with flour and roll out the dough to an 8 mm (⅜ inch) thickness. Cut the biscuits into 4 cm (1½ inch) squares. Using a small knife, pick up each biscuit and place it on the prepared tray approximately 1.5 cm (⅝ inch) apart, as they will spread a little during baking. (Instead of rolling out the biscuit dough you can simply use a teaspoon and spoon small amounts onto the lined tray.) Bake for 9–10 minutes. Remove from the oven and leave on the tray to cool at room temperature.

GARNISH

60 g (2¼ oz) pecans
250 g (9 oz/1⅔ cups) coarsely chopped good-quality dark chocolate

Preheat the oven to 160°C (315°F). Put the pecans on a baking tray and roast them for 8–10 minutes. Set aside to cool completely.

Temper the chocolate (see pages 12–14). Once the biscuits are cool, dip the top in the chocolate and immediately place a cooled roasted pecan on top. Leave at room temperature to set. These biscuits are best eaten within a week and stored at room temperature in an airtight container. If your room temperature is warm, store them in the refrigerator in an airtight container.

COCONUT CHOCOLATE BISCUITS

MAKES: 36 DIFFICULTY: ◼ **GLUTEN-FREE**

Coconut and chocolate make a great pair in this recipe, which is an adaptation of the classic coconut macaroon. I dip these into dark chocolate, but you can also enjoy them without the chocolate finish. Also, the mixed peel can be interchanged with diced glacé cherries.

COCONUT CHOCOLATE BISCUITS

75 g (2¾ oz/about 3) egg whites

pinch of cream of tartar

150 g (5½ oz/⅔ cup) caster (superfine) sugar

15 g (½ oz) hazelnut meal

10 g (⅜ oz) Dutch-process cocoa powder

15 g (½ oz) mixed peel (mixed candied citrus peel)

90 g (3¼ oz/1 cup) desiccated (shredded) coconut

50 g (1¾ oz) good-quality milk chocolate chips, coarsely chopped

Preheat the oven to 170°C (325°F) and line a baking tray with a non-stick mat or baking paper. Using an electric mixer with a whisk attachment, beat the egg whites and cream of tartar on high speed until medium peaks form. Gradually add the caster sugar and continue mixing for 1 minute to ensure the sugar dissolves. Using a spatula, fold through the hazelnut meal and sieved cocoa powder by hand, followed by the mixed peel, coconut and chocolate chips. Transfer the prepared mixture to a piping (icing) bag with a 1.5 cm (⅝ inch) plain nozzle. Pipe individual 3 cm (1¼ inch) mounds onto the lined tray, approximately 2 cm (¾ inch) apart. Bake for 8–10 minutes, until crunchy. Leave on the tray to cool at room temperature. Remove from the tray once completely cooled.

GARNISH

small block dark chocolate

200 g (7 oz/1⅓ cups) coarsely chopped good-quality dark chocolate

Take a knife with a straight blade and scrape the flat surface of the chocolate block to create chocolate shavings. Create enough to fill a medium bowl.

Temper the chopped chocolate (see pages 12–14). Once the biscuits are cool, using a fork or toothpicks, dip a macaroon in the prepared tempered chocolate and place it directly into the chocolate shavings. Using a spoon, cover the macaroon completely in chocolate shavings and ensure the chocolate sets on each macaroon completely before removing it from the bowl of shavings. Repeat with the remaining macaroons. (These macaroons can also be eaten as they are, without the additional chocolate.) These biscuits are best eaten within 2 weeks and stored at room temperature in an airtight container. If your room temperature is warm, store them in the refrigerator in an airtight container.

CHOCOLATE CHIP COOKIES

MAKES: 50   DIFFICULTY: 🍫

It's best that you don't over-bake these cookies, so they'll retain a slightly fudgy texture in the centre. The cookie dough can be frozen in individual portions and baked as needed.

150 g (5½ oz) unsalted butter
160 g (5½ oz) soft brown sugar
¼ teaspoon vanilla bean paste
120 g (4¼ oz/about 2) whole eggs
230 g (8 oz) plain (all-purpose) flour
1 teaspoon baking powder
½ teaspoon ground cinnamon
200 g (7 oz) good-quality milk chocolate chips
25 g (1 oz) good-quality dark chocolate chips

Preheat the oven to 170°C (325°F) and line a baking tray with a non-stick mat or baking paper. Using an electric mixer with a paddle attachment, cream the butter, brown sugar and vanilla bean paste on medium speed. Add the eggs, mixing well and scraping down the side of the bowl as necessary. Add the flour, baking powder and cinnamon and mix to combine. Add the chocolate chips (if they are too large, roughly chop them) and mix until just combined – stop mixing so you don't crush the chocolate chips too much.

Scoop teaspoonfuls of the cookie mixture onto the lined tray, leaving a 2 cm (¾ inch) gap between the cookies. Ensure all the cookies are of a similar size so they bake evenly. Bake for 8–10 minutes. Remove from the oven, transfer to a wire rack and cool at room temperature. Store in an airtight container at room temperature for up to 2 weeks.

DECADENT CHOCOLATE BISCUITS

MAKES: 32 DIFFICULTY: 🍫🍫

The name of the recipe says it all – these are decadent little morsels.
You can bake the biscuits in advance and store them for two weeks.
Once you add the ganache they'll only have a four-day shelf life.

45 g (1½ oz) caster (superfine) sugar
45 g (1½ oz/1½ cups) roasted corn
  flakes cereal
½ teaspoon unsalted butter

CARAMELISED PUFFED CORN FLAKES

Line a tray with a non-stick mat or baking paper. Put the sugar and 15 ml (½ fl oz/3 teaspoons) water in a saucepan over medium heat and bring to 114°C (237°F). (If you don't have a sugar thermometer, take a small amount of syrup out of the saucepan with a teaspoon and drop it into a bowl of cold water – if it's the right temperature it will make a soft pliable ball when you remove it from the water and squeeze it between your fingers.) Remove the pan from the heat and add the roasted corn flakes. Mix, off the heat, until the sugar turns from a liquid to sugar crystals again around the corn flakes. Put the pan back over low heat and, while stirring, gently melt and caramelise the sugar. Once the sugar is fully melted and caramelised, add the butter. Immediately scrape the mixture onto the prepared tray and spread it out with a fork. Leave to cool at room temperature. Once cool, break it into smaller pieces. Store in an airtight container until required.

60 g (2¼ oz/⅓ cup lightly packed) soft brown sugar
100 g (3½ oz) caster (superfine) sugar
115 g (4 oz) unsalted butter
60 g (2¼ oz/about 1) whole egg
1 teaspoon vanilla bean paste
250 g (9 oz/1⅔ cups) plain (all-purpose) flour
20 g (¾ oz) cornflour (cornstarch)
¼ teaspoon bicarbonate of soda (baking soda)
¼ teaspoon baking powder
pinch of salt
150 g (5½ oz) milk chocolate chips, finely chopped if large
150 g (5½ oz) dark chocolate chips, finely chopped if large
caramelised puffed corn flakes (see opposite)

220 g (7¾ oz) good-quality dark chocolate, coarsely chopped
30 g (1 oz) good-quality milk chocolate, coarsely chopped
250 ml (9 fl oz/1 cup) cream (35% fat)

CORNFLAKE CHOCOLATE BISCUITS

Preheat the oven to 170°C (325°F) and line a baking tray with a non-stick mat or baking paper. Using an electric mixer with a paddle attachment, beat the brown sugar, caster sugar and butter on medium speed until all the lumps of butter have been incorporated and the mixture is light and creamy. (Alternatively, you can mix by hand.) Add the egg and vanilla bean paste and mix to combine. Sift in the flour, cornflour, bicarbonate of soda, baking powder and salt and mix to combine, then mix in the chocolate chips and caramelised puffed corn flakes. Place 2.5 cm (1 inch) balls on the prepared tray, 2 cm (¾ inch) apart. Bake for 8–10 minutes, until golden. Leave to cool on the tray at room temperature.

CHOCOLATE GANACHE

Put the chocolates in a bowl. Put the cream in a small saucepan over medium heat and bring to the boil. Pour the hot cream over the chocolate, whisking until the chocolate has melted to create a ganache. Cover the surface of the ganache with plastic wrap. Leave to cool at room temperature for approximately 1 hour, or until it reaches piping consistency. When you press gently on the plastic and the ganache has a firm but pliable consistency, it's ready to pipe. Transfer to a piping (icing) bag with a 1 cm (½ inch) plain nozzle.

ASSEMBLY

Once the biscuits are cool, turn over every second biscuit. If you have varied sizes, match them into like-sized pairs. Pipe the ganache onto one side of the pair, or use a teaspoon to scoop on small amounts of ganache. Pick the base up and match it with its pair then press the two gently together. These biscuits can be stored in an airtight container for up to 4 days at room temperature.

Decadent Chocolate Biscuits PAGE 28

Chocolate Gingerbread
Caramel Biscuits PAGE 32

CHOCOLATE GINGERBREAD CARAMEL BISCUITS

MAKES: 24   DIFFICULTY: 🍫

You can make these cute biscuits in any shape or size you like. I prefer it if they are assembled not too far in advance before eating them.

10 g (⅜ oz) gingerbread spice (or see gingerbread spice recipe on opposite page)

270 g (9½ oz) plain (all-purpose) flour, plus extra for dusting

30 g (1 oz/¼ cup) Dutch-process cocoa powder

135 g (4¾ oz) honey

85 g (3 oz) caster (superfine) sugar

20 g (¾ oz) unsalted butter, softened

1 teaspoon salt

½ teaspoon bicarbonate of soda (baking soda)

45 ml (1½ fl oz) boiling water

CHOCOLATE GINGERBREAD

Sift the spice, flour and cocoa powder into the bowl of an electric mixer with a paddle attachment. Add the honey, sugar, butter and salt and beat on medium speed until there are no lumps of butter in the mix.

Put the bicarbonate of soda and boiling water in a bowl and mix to combine. (This process will release a lot of the gasses the baking soda creates, so your biscuit will bake more evenly.) Add the baking soda mixture to the ingredients in the mixer bowl and continue mixing until a dough forms. Press the dough into an even, flat square, wrap it in plastic wrap and place it in the refrigerator to rest for 20–30 minutes.

Preheat the oven to 170°C (325°F) and line a baking tray with a non-stick mat or baking paper. Lightly dust a work surface with flour and roll out the dough to a 4 mm (3/16 inch) thickness. Using a 5 cm (2 inch) heart-shaped cutter (or other shape), cut out 24 bases and place them 2 cm (¾ inches) apart on the lined tray. Re-roll the pastry if needed, and cut out an additional 24 hearts. Using a smaller heart-shaped cutter, cut a smaller heart from the centre of the second batch of hearts to create a heart-shaped hole. Brush water around the edge of the gingerbread base and apply the second heart frame on top, pressing it on gently. Bake for approximately 7 minutes, until golden. Remove the biscuits from the oven and leave to cool on the tray at room temperature.

GINGERBREAD SPICE

1 teaspoon ground cinnamon

1 teaspoon ground cloves

¼ teaspoon ground allspice

⅓ teaspoon ground nutmeg

¼ teaspoon ground coriander

¼ teaspoon ground cardamom

¼ teaspoon ground ginger

¼ teaspoon ground anise seed

If you can't source gingerbread spice, also called German gingerbread spice or lebkuchen spice, you can create your own spice mix by combining these spices together. Store the mixture in the freezer until required. Alternatively replace the gingerbread spice with mixed spice.

CARAMEL FILLING

100 ml (3½ fl oz) cream (35% fat)

1 teaspoon vanilla bean paste

1 teaspoon sea salt

zest of 1 orange

130 g (4½ oz) caster (superfine) sugar

30 g (1 oz/1 tablespoon) liquid glucose

220 g (7¾ oz) unsalted butter

Put the cream, vanilla bean paste, salt and orange zest in a saucepan over medium heat and bring to the boil. Cover and keep warm.

Put the sugar in a large heavy-based saucepan over low heat and stir gently until the sugar is completely dissolved, caramelised and dark golden in colour. Remove the pan from the heat and, while whisking, add the hot vanilla cream to stop the caramel cooking. (Be careful when adding the cream as it will generate a lot of steam and increase in volume very quickly.) Add the glucose and butter and whisk until combined. Strain this mixture into a bowl and cover the caramel with plastic wrap so that it is touching the surface (this will help to prevent getting a skin on the caramel). Leave the caramel in its original bowl at room temperature (over-stirring it or agitation can cause the caramel to crystallise). It can be made up to a week in advance.

ASSEMBLY

Once the caramel is cool and you are ready to pipe, place the caramel in a piping (icing) bag with a small plain nozzle and pipe the caramel (or use a spoon), to fill the centre of the cooled biscuits. These can be stored flat in an airtight container for up to 4 days. If kept separate, the biscuits and caramel can be stored in airtight containers for up to a week at room temperature.

PEANUT BUTTER COOKIES

MAKES: 45 DIFFICULTY: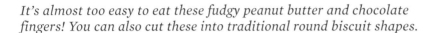

It's almost too easy to eat these fudgy peanut butter and chocolate fingers! You can also cut these into traditional round biscuit shapes.

95 g (3¼ oz) unsalted butter

60 g (2¼ oz/⅓ cup lightly packed) soft brown sugar

60 g (2¼ oz) caster (superfine) sugar

90 g (3¼ oz) crunchy peanut butter

30 g (1 oz/about ½) whole egg

125 g (4½ oz) plain (all-purpose) flour, plus extra for dusting

pinch of baking powder

pinch of salt

75 g (2¾ oz) milk chocolate chips, coarsely chopped

Using an electric mixer with a paddle attachment, cream the butter and sugars on medium speed until the butter is fully incorporated and lumps of butter are no longer visible. Add the peanut butter followed by the egg and the remaining ingredients, except the chocolate, and mix to just combine. Finally, add the chopped chocolate chips. As soon as the mixture comes together as a dough, stop mixing. Press the dough into an even, flat square, wrap it in plastic wrap and place it in the refrigerator to rest for 20–30 minutes.

Preheat the oven to 170°C (325°F) and line a baking tray with a non-stick mat or baking paper. Lightly dust a work surface with flour and roll the dough out to a 4 mm (³⁄₁₆ inch) thickness. Cut the dough into 7 x 2 cm (2¾ x ¾ inch) rectangles. Pick the biscuits up with a spatula and place them on the lined tray, about 1 cm (½ inch) apart. Bake for approximately 7–8 minutes. Leave to cool on the tray at room temperature. Store in an airtight container for up to 1 month.

FLORENTINES

MAKES: 36 DIFFICULTY: ♦♦ **GLUTEN-FREE**

You'll find these florentines hard to resist! I love to give these as a gift at Christmas time. If you prefer, the nuts and seeds can be interchanged with alternative nuts as long as you keep the same weight.

125 g (4½ oz) caster (superfine) sugar

75 ml (2½ fl oz) cream (35% fat)

40 g (1½ oz) honey

35 g (1¼ oz) liquid glucose

60 g (2¼ oz) unsalted butter

100 g (3½ oz) flaked almonds

50 g (1¾ oz) pistachio nuts, slivered
   or roughly chopped

50 g (1¾ oz/⅓ cup) sesame seeds

75 g (2¾ oz/½ cup) hazelnuts, chopped

25 g (1 oz) glacé cherries, sliced

230 g (8 oz) good-quality milk chocolate,
   coarsely chopped

Preheat the oven to 170°C (325°F) and line a baking tray with a non-stick mat or baking paper. Heat the caster sugar, cream, honey, glucose and butter in a saucepan over medium heat and bring to the boil. Cook until you achieve a light golden colour. Remove the pan from the heat and add the remaining ingredients, except the milk chocolate, and stir to combine.

Place 3 cm (1¼ inch) rounds of the mixture on the lined tray 10 cm (4 inches) apart and bake for 8–10 minutes or until golden brown. Remove the tray from the oven and, while the florentines are still hot, take a 7 cm (2¾ inch) cutter or overturned cup, and place it over a baked hot florentine. With a continual circular motion, neaten the edges of each florentine to create an even round disc. (This is optional, they taste just as good with uneven edges.) Leave to cool completely on the tray. Once cool, remove from the tray.

Temper the chocolate (see pages 12–14). To coat the bases with the tempered chocolate, dip a small knife or the back of a spoon into the chocolate and spread a thin layer onto the bases of the florentines. Leave them, chocolate side up, at room temperature until the chocolate has set. Keep the florentines in a sealed bag or airtight container for up to 4 weeks. If your room temperature is warm, store them in the refrigerator in an airtight container.

CHOCOLATE MACARONS

MAKES: 70 DIFFICULTY: 🍫🍫 **GLUTEN-FREE**

Macarons can be challenging to perfect, so here are some handy tips: use egg whites that have been cracked at least 24 hours in advance and left at room temperature before whisking; when mixing the macaron mixture, if you let it sit for 2 minutes on the work surface prior to piping, it should just level out in the bowl; it's important not to over-mix or your macarons will be flat; draw 3 cm (1¼ inch) rings onto a sheet of baking paper and turn it over onto a baking tray to use as a guide for piping; Once piped, put the trays immediately into the oven.

CHOCOLATE MACARONS

330 g (11½ oz) icing (confectioners') sugar

320 g (11¼ oz) almond meal

125 g (4½ oz/about 5) egg whites (a)

15 g (½ oz) Dutch-process cocoa powder

330 g (11½ oz/1½ cups) caster (superfine) sugar

125 g (4½ oz/about 5) egg whites (b)

pinch of cream of tartar

brown oil-based powdered food colouring

Preheat the oven to 150°C (300°F) and line a baking tray with a non-stick mat or baking paper. Combine the icing sugar and almond meal in a food processor to create a fine powder and sieve the mixture into a bowl. Add the egg whites (a) and cocoa powder and combine to make a dense chocolate almond paste.

In a small saucepan over medium heat create a syrup by heating 85 ml (2¾ fl oz) water and the caster sugar to 118°C (244°F). (If you don't have a sugar thermometer, use a teaspoon to take a small amount of the sugar syrup as it's cooking and drop it into a bowl of cold water. When it reaches the correct temperature, the sugar will create a pliable ball when you pick it up.)

When the sugar syrup starts to boil, slowly whisk the egg whites (b) and cream of tartar using an electric mixer with a whisk attachment on medium speed until medium peaks form. When the sugar syrup reaches the correct temperature, pour the syrup down the side of the bowl into the egg whites, trying not to let the syrup touch the moving whisk. Add small amounts of brown food colouring until it reaches a dark chocolate brown colour. Continue whisking the meringue until it cools to approximately 50°C (122°F).

Fold half of the completed meringue into the almond paste mixture with a firm spatula until combined then add the remaining meringue, mixing until the paste is supple and shiny. Transfer the mixture to a piping (icing) bag with a 1 cm (½ inch) plain nozzle.

Pipe 3 cm (1¼ inch) discs of macaron onto the lined tray then bake for 15 minutes. To check when the macaron shells are ready, open the oven door and move a shell from side to side gently. If it's ready, the shell will be firm but still secured to the lined tray. Remove the shells from the oven and leave them on the tray to cool completely. The shells at this stage can be frozen for up to 1 month. ☞

1. Combine the macaron mixture with a firm spatula or scraper.

2. Letting the macaron mixture sit for 2 minutes on the work surface prior to piping it should level it out.

3. Draw 3 cm (1¼ inch) rings onto baking paper and turn it over or use it as a guide underneath a baking mat for piping.

4. Pipe the prepared ganache filling onto every second macaron.

5. Gently join two macarons together.

CHOCOLATE GANACHE FILLING

360 g (12¾ oz) good-quality dark
   chocolate, coarsely chopped
270 ml (9½ fl oz) cream (35% fat)
20 g (¾ oz) Dutch-process cocoa
   powder
½ teaspoon sea salt

Put the chocolate in a bowl. Put the cream, cocoa powder and salt in a medium saucepan over medium heat and bring to the boil. Pour the mixture over the dark chocolate, whisking by hand until the chocolate is melted and combined – it should have a shiny, supple finish. Cover with plastic wrap touching the surface. Leave at room temperature for approximately 2 hours to set to a piping consistency (this time may vary depending on your room temperature – it should feel firm but pliable). Place the ganache in a piping (icing) bag with a 1 cm (½ inch) plain nozzle. (Alternatively, you can spoon the ganache filling onto the macaron shells.)

Turn over every second macaron shell and, if you have varied sizes, match them into like-sized pairs. Pipe the ganache onto 1 shell of the pair. Place the second macaron shell on top and gently press them together. These macarons can be stored in the refrigerator for up to 4 days or frozen for up to 1 month.

CHOCOLATE FUDGE WHEELS

MAKES: 42   DIFFICULTY: ◆◆◆

If you're up for the challenge, these fudge wheels are well worth the effort. Although they're the most challenging biscuit in the chapter, they're also one of the most delicious.

CHOCOLATE PASTRY

185 g (6½ oz) unsalted butter

100 g (3½ oz) icing (confectioners') sugar

20 g (¾ oz) Dutch-process cocoa powder

80 g (2¾ oz/about 4) egg yolks

pinch of salt

305 g (10¾ oz) plain (all-purpose) flour, plus extra for dusting

1 teaspoon baking powder

110 g (3¾ oz/¾ cup) coarsely chopped good-quality dark chocolate

Using an electric mixer with a paddle attachment, cream the butter, icing sugar and cocoa powder on medium speed. Add the egg yolks, mixing well and scraping down the side of the bowl as necessary. Add the remaining ingredients, except the chocolate, and mix just until the pastry comes together as a dough. Press the dough into an even, flat square, wrap it in plastic wrap and place it in the refrigerator to rest for 30–45 minutes, until firm.

Preheat the oven to 180°C (350°F) and line a baking tray with a non-stick mat or baking paper. Remove the dough from the refrigerator and roll it out on a lightly floured work surface to a 4 mm (³/₁₆ inch) thickness. Using a 5 cm (2 inch) round cutter, cut out individual discs. Place the discs onto the lined tray and bake for 5–6 minutes. Remove from the oven and leave on the tray to cool completely at room temperature.

In a plastic bowl in the microwave, melt the dark chocolate to body temperature in 20–30-second bursts on high (100%). Stir the melted chocolate vigorously then spread it onto the flat surface of each biscuit. Leave at room temperature to set.

SALTED CARAMEL

70 ml (2¼ fl oz) cream (35% fat)

pinch of sea salt

100 g (3½ oz) caster (superfine) sugar

80 g (2¾ oz) unsalted butter, chopped

Put the cream and salt in a small saucepan over medium heat and bring to the boil. Set aside. Put the sugar in a large heavy-based saucepan and stir gently over medium heat until the sugar fully dissolves and caramelises. Turn off the heat and stop the caramel cooking by immediately pouring the cream over the caramel. Whisk to combine, then add the butter a piece at a time and whisk to incorporate. Pour the caramel into a bowl and place plastic wrap on top so it comes in direct contact with the caramel. Leave at room temperature to cool completely. ☞

I. Spread a thin layer of chocolate onto the base of each biscuit.

2. Pipe the chocolate fudge cream carefully around the edge of every second biscuit.

3. Fill the centre with caramel.

CHOCOLATE FUDGE CREAM

200 g (7 oz/1⅓ cups) finely chopped good-quality dark chocolate
200 ml (7 fl oz) cream (35% fat)
pinch of salt
¼ teaspoon vanilla bean paste
125 g (4½ oz) unsalted butter, softened

Put the chocolate in a bowl. Put the cream, salt and vanilla bean paste in a saucepan over medium heat and bring to the boil. Pour the hot cream mixture over the chocolate and whisk to combine until the chocolate is completely melted, to create a ganache. Place plastic wrap on the surface of the ganache and leave to cool at room temperature.

Once the ganache has cooled down, put the butter in the bowl of an electric mixer with a whisk attachment and mix on high speed. Slowly add the ganache, whisking until combined, light and creamy. If the mixture becomes too soft, place it in the refrigerator and whip again once the mixture becomes firm. The mixture may separate but it will come back together once whipped.

ASSEMBLY

Put the chocolate fudge cream in a piping (icing) bag with a 1 cm (½ inch) plain nozzle. Pipe a ring of the chocolate fudge cream around the edge of every second biscuit, on top of the dark chocolate, leaving space in the centre for the salted caramel.

Place the salted caramel in a piping bag (with no nozzle), or use a spoon, and fill the centre of each biscuit, just until it is level with the fudge cream. Immediately place a second biscuit on top, chocolate side down, and gently press together without pushing the cream out.

FINISHING

400 g (14 oz/2⅔ cups) coarsely chopped good-quality milk chocolate
Dutch-process cocoa powder, for dusting

Temper the chocolate (see pages 12–14). Crumple up a piece of baking paper and then flatten it out. Repeat this process three times. Spread the paper out flat and sieve a very fine dust of cocoa powder on the surface. Place the prepared biscuits on a fork and dip them in the tempered chocolate. Wipe the excess chocolate off the base of the biscuit on the side of the bowl. (If the dipping process feels unstable, you can press a toothpick on the top of the biscuit as you dip it.) Place the dipped biscuit onto the cocoa powder–lined baking paper. Leave to set at room temperature for 20–30 minutes. These biscuits will keep in an airtight container for up to 2 weeks.

4. *Place the second biscuit on top and sandwich together.*

5. *Lightly dust a crumpled piece of baking paper with cocoa powder.*

6. *Dip the biscuit in milk chocolate before placing on the prepared baking paper.*

HAZELNUT CHOCOLATE BISCUITS

MAKES: 65   DIFFICULTY: ◼◼◼   **GLUTEN-FREE**

Although these decadent biscuits require more time than most, you'll be rewarded with a delicious and indulgent treat. This recipe makes a large quantity of biscuits, as it is difficult to whisk smaller quantities of egg white in the dacquoise recipe – but I promise they'll all be gone in no time! I designed this one for my sister Fiona who has as much love for chocolate as me.

110 g (3¾ oz) hazelnuts

50 g (1¾ oz/about 2) egg whites

60 g (2¼ oz) caster (superfine) sugar

⅛ teaspoon cream of tartar

30 g (1 oz/¼ cup) hazelnut meal

20 g (¾ oz) almond meal

60 g (2¼ oz/½ cup) icing (confectioners')
   sugar, plus extra for dusting

30 g (1 oz/¼ cup) cornflour (cornstarch)

HAZELNUT DACQUOISE BISCUIT

Preheat the oven to 160°C (315°F). Put the hazelnuts on a baking tray lined with baking paper and bake for 12–15 minutes or until fully roasted. Rub the roasted nuts with a cloth to remove the skins. Roughly chop the nuts, divide them evenly into three bowls and set aside.

Using an electric mixer with a whisk attachment, whisk the egg whites, half the caster sugar and the cream of tartar on medium speed until soft peaks form. Gradually add the remaining caster sugar and continue mixing for 1 minute or until the sugar is dissolved.

Sift the hazelnut meal, almond meal, icing sugar and cornflour together into a bowl. (If all the meal doesn't go through the sieve, you can still add the larger pieces of nuts to the sifted ingredients.) Fold the sifted dry ingredients into the meringue base. Transfer the prepared meringue mixture into a piping (icing) bag with a 1 cm (½ inch) plain nozzle.

If you like, you can make yourself a piping guide by drawing 3 cm (1¼ inch) circles on a sheet of baking paper, approximately 1.5 cm (⅝ inch) apart, and then turning it over to use as a guide.

Pipe 3 cm (1¼ inch) discs in a coil shape, starting from the centre and working outwards or spread the dacquoise out with a teaspoon to the same diameter. Sprinkle the dacquoise with one-third of the chopped hazelnuts. Dust the surface of the dacquoise lightly with icing sugar. Bake for 20–25 minutes, until golden and crunchy on the outside. Leave on the tray and cool at room temperature. Remove them from the tray once cool. The dacquoise will be crunchy on the outside and chewy in the centre. These can be eaten on their own. You can store these separately in an airtight container at room temperature for up to 1 week. 👉

CHOCOLATE GANACHE

235 g (8½ oz) good-quality dark
chocolate, coarsely chopped
60 g (2¼ oz/2 tablespoons) honey
400 ml (14 fl oz) cream (35% fat)
30 g (1 oz/1 tablespoon) liquid glucose
20 g (¾ oz) unsalted butter

Put the chocolate and honey in a bowl. Put the cream and glucose in a saucepan over medium heat and bring to the boil. Immediately pour the hot cream mixture over the dark chocolate and honey and combine with a hand-held blender or whisk by hand. Once the chocolate has melted, add the butter and continue mixing to create a ganache. Cover with plastic wrap touching the surface and leave at room temperature for 5 hours. To speed up the process of the ganache setting, you can spread it on a tray lined with plastic wrap, with a second sheet of plastic wrap on top of the ganache, then leave it at room temperature.

Once the ganache feels firm enough to pipe, place it in a piping (icing) bag with a 1 cm (½ inch) plain nozzle. Pipe coils of ganache onto the baked biscuits, starting from the centre of each dacquoise and working outwards, not extending the ganache beyond the edge. Alternatively, you can spoon the ganache on. If the ganache is left too long, it will be too firm to spread or pipe. Keep the dacquoise and ganache at room temperature.

1. Pipe the prepared dacquoise onto your prepared baking tray.

2. Place one-third of the hazelnuts on top prior to baking.

3. Pipe the prepared ganache on top of the baked biscuits.

4. *Place one-third of the hazelnuts on top and dip the biscuits in milk chocolate.*

5. *Garnish with the remaining hazelnuts.*

FINISHING

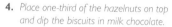

600 g (1 lb 5 oz) good-quality milk chocolate

Sprinkle one-third of the roasted chopped hazelnuts onto the piped ganache and press them slightly into the surface.

Temper the chocolate (see pages 12–14). Place the biscuits onto a fork and dip them in the tempered chocolate. Wipe the excess chocolate off the base of the biscuit on the side of the bowl. (If the dipping process feels unstable, you can press a toothpick into the top of the filling as you dip it.) Place the dipped biscuit down onto a sheet of baking paper and sprinkle the top with the remaining roasted hazelnuts. Leave to set at room temperature (your room temperature must be below 23°C/73°F for the chocolate to set or you will have to set it in the refrigerator). These biscuits are best eaten within a week and stored at room temperature in an airtight container. If your room temperature is warm, store them in the refrigerator in an airtight container.

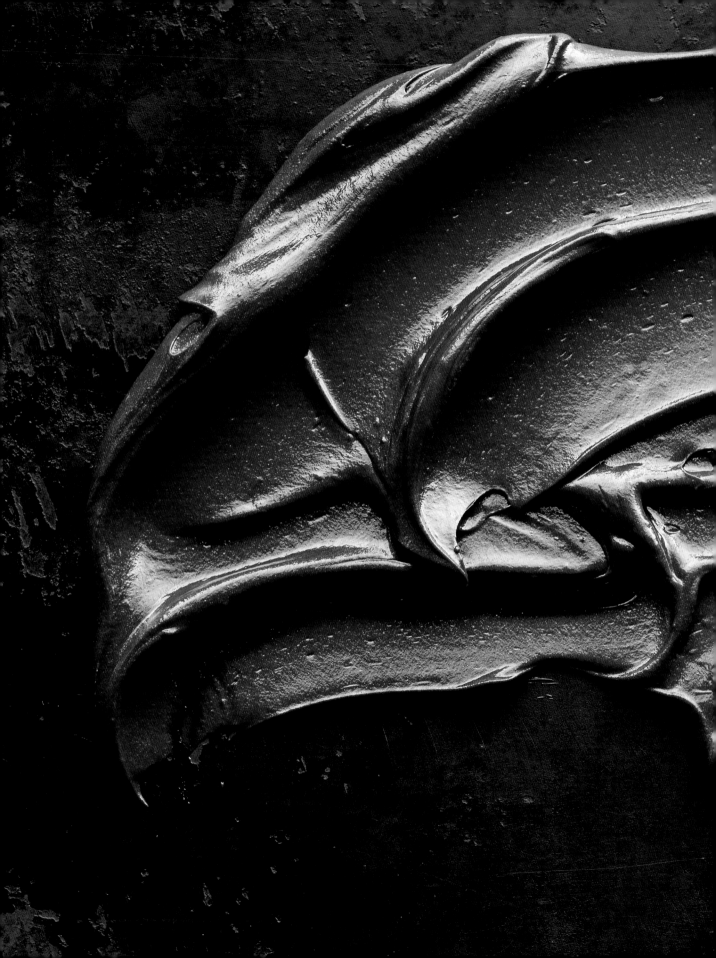

2.
CHOCOLATES

CHOCOLATE-COATED HONEYCOMB

SERVES: 6-8   DIFFICULTY: ◆ **GLUTEN-FREE**

Honeycomb is simple to make but there are a few tips to ensure you end up with a perfect result every time. When adding the bicarbonate of soda, just whisk it until combined or else you'll knock out all the air. The honeycomb needs to be coated in chocolate shortly after it has cooled to avoid it absorbing moisture and going soft.

225 g (8 oz) caster (superfine) sugar

55 g (2 oz) honey

85 g (3 oz) liquid glucose

10 g (⅜ oz/2 teaspoons) bicarbonate of soda (baking soda), sifted

480 g (1 lb 1 oz) good-quality milk chocolate, coarsely chopped

Place a large sheet of baking paper on a heatproof surface. Put the sugar, honey, glucose and 40 ml (1¼ fl oz/2 tablespoons) water in a saucepan over medium heat and stir until it starts to boil. Once boiling, stop stirring the mixture. When the temperature reaches 157°C (315°F) — if you don't have a sugar thermometer the bubbles on the surface should reach a light golden colour — add the sifted bicarbonate of soda and whisk just a few times to incorporate. Pour the honeycomb mixture onto the baking paper and don't move it until it is cold.

Temper the chocolate (see pages 12–14). Break up the honeycomb into small pieces and mix it through the tempered chocolate until well coated. Spread the chocolate-coated honeycomb on a tray lined with baking paper and leave at room temperature to set. If your room temperature is too warm, place in a sealed container in the refrigerator. Break up the honeycomb sheet into large chunks and serve or wrap in cellophane or sealed packaging to present as a gift. This has a 4-week shelf life if left in a single sheet. Once broken up, it will need to be eaten within a few days.

ALMOND BON BONS

MAKES: 10 **DIFFICULTY:** ⬛ GLUTEN-FREE

Bon bons — a French term translating to 'good goods' — is the perfect title for these Christmas-inspired chocolates. They make perfect little gifts that are guaranteed to please family and friends.

ROASTED SLIVERED ALMONDS

60 g (2¼ oz) caster (superfine) sugar
250 g (9 oz/2 cups) slivered almonds

Preheat the oven to 160°C (315°F) and line a baking tray with a non-stick mat or baking paper. Put the sugar and 25 ml (¾ fl oz) water in a saucepan over medium heat and bring to the boil. Cook just until the sugar is dissolved. Put the almonds in a bowl and pour the sugar syrup over them, mixing to combine. Spread the coated almonds on the prepared tray and bake for approximately 10–12 minutes, stirring the nuts every few minutes to ensure that they bake evenly. Continue baking until the almonds are golden brown and all the syrup has evaporated. Set the almonds aside on the tray to cool at room temperature.

CHOCOLATE ALMONDS

roasted slivered almonds (recipe above)
50 g (1¾ oz) pistachio nuts, roughly chopped
100 g (3½ oz) mixed peel (mixed candied citrus peel)
25 g (1 oz/1 cup) puffed rice cereal
350 g (12 oz) good-quality white chocolate, coarsely chopped

Cut ten 20 x 11 cm (8 x 4¼ inch) rectangles of acetate. Roll each piece from a short side into a tube, approximately 3.5 cm (1½ inches) in diameter and tape them to secure. Stand the tubes up on a tray lined with baking paper.

Put the cooled, prepared roasted almonds in a bowl with the pistachio nuts, mixed peel and puffed rice cereal. Temper the chocolate (see pages 12–14). Mix the tempered chocolate through the dry ingredients until everything is well coated. Using a teaspoon, fill each tube with the mixture. Place the tubes down flat on the tray and then place in the refrigerator for 10–15 minutes to set. Once set, unroll each tube and wrap in cellophane with additional cellophane overhanging at the ends. Tie the ends with ribbon and if necessary secure the bon bons with a small piece of clear tape in the centre. These are best stored at room temperature. They have a long shelf life of 3 months. You can interchange the white chocolate for milk or dark, but you will have to work quickly as it will set faster.

MILK CHOCOLATE HONEY TRUFFLES

MAKES: 40 DIFFICULTY: ◆ **GLUTEN-FREE**

If there were ever a food product that required high security, these truffles are it! Although the recipe yields forty truffles, don't be suprised if they don't last beyond one sitting. Truffles make excellent gifts too – if you can bear to part with them!

170 g (6 oz) flaked almonds, roasted

300 g (10½ oz) good-quality milk chocolate (a)

125 ml (4 fl oz/½ cup) cream (35% fat)

15 g (½ oz/2 teaspoons) honey

1 vanilla bean, seeds scraped

300 g (10½ oz) good-quality milk chocolate (b)

edible gold metallic or lustre powder (optional)

Preheat the oven to 160°C (315°F). Place the flaked almonds on a baking tray lined with baking paper and roast for approximately 10–15 minutes until golden brown. Leave at room temperature to cool and then store in an airtight container until required.

Put the chocolate (a) in a bowl. Put the cream, honey and vanilla bean seeds in a saucepan over medium heat and bring to the boil. Pour the hot cream over the chocolate (a), whisking by hand to create a ganache. Continue mixing until all the chocolate is combined and the ganache is supple and shiny. Scrape the ganache down the side of the bowl and cover the bowl with plastic wrap so it touches the surface of the ganache. Store at room temperature for a minimum of 5 hours, or until it feels firm but pliable when you press on the ganache. If your room temperature is over 23°C (73°F), place the ganache in the refrigerator for a short period just until it firms up enough to pipe.

Once the ganache is firm, transfer it to a piping (icing) bag with a 1.2 cm (7/16 inch) plain nozzle and pipe round dollops, approximately 2 cm (¾ inch) in diameter, onto a flat tray lined with baking paper. (You can also use a teaspoon to scoop small amounts onto a lined tray.) Leave the ganache balls at room temperature (not above 23°C/73°F) until they form a skin on the surface. This should take approximately 1 hour. Roll the ganache balls between your palms to create spheres. Do this as quickly as possible so the ganache doesn't melt. Let the truffles sit at room temperature for 1 hour.

Spread the almonds out onto a tray and crush them slightly. Temper the chocolate (b) (see pages 12–14). Coat your fingers in the milk chocolate and roll each truffle in your fingers as quickly as possible so it is completely coated in chocolate. Drop the coated truffle into the crushed almonds and then roll each truffle through the almonds, using a fork until coated. (It's a good idea to have a helper to coat the truffles in the almonds.) Leave each truffle in the almonds for 10 minutes to set before removing. If desired, lightly dust each truffle with gold metallic or lustre powder. These truffles are best stored at room temperature or, if your room temperature exceeds 23°C (73°F), stored in a sealed container in the refrigerator, for up to 8 days.

WHITE COCONUT TRUFFLES

MAKES: 100 DIFFICULTY: ◆ **GLUTEN-FREE**

I love the flavour of coconut, and combined with a dark chocolate coating it is hard to beat. These are perfect served with afternoon tea or as a petit four after dinner.

350 g (12 oz) good-quality white chocolate, finely chopped

90 ml (3 fl oz) coconut milk

35 g (1¼ oz) desiccated (shredded) coconut, plus extra for rolling

15 ml (½ fl oz/3 teaspoons) coconut liqueur

750 g (1 lb 10 oz/5 cups) coarsely chopped good-quality dark chocolate

Half-melt the white chocolate in a double boiler or in a plastic bowl in the microwave (see page 12). Put the coconut milk in a saucepan over medium heat and bring to the boil. Pour the hot coconut milk over the partially melted white chocolate and whisk vigorously by hand until the chocolate is melted. Add the desiccated coconut and coconut liqueur and whisk to combine to create a ganache. Transfer to a piping (icing) bag with a 1.2 cm (⁷⁄₁₆ inch) plain nozzle.

Pipe long strips of the ganache across the length of a tray lined with baking paper, or just spoon the mixture on if you don't have a piping bag. Leave the ganache at room temperature for 5–6 hours until firm. If your room temperature is too warm, place in the refrigerator for no more than 30 minutes. Cut the ganache into 3 cm (1¼ inch) lengths and separate them.

Temper the dark chocolate (see pages 12–14). Scatter some extra desiccated coconut onto a tray. Using a fork, dip each truffle in the dark chocolate, tap it to remove any excess chocolate and then wipe the base of the fork on the bowl before placing the truffle in the tray of coconut. (It will be easier if you have a helper to roll the truffles in the coconut.) Leave each truffle to set for 5–7 minutes before removing it from the coconut. Reheat your chocolate as needed with a hair dryer. These truffles are best stored at room temperature (not exceeding 23°C/73°F) for up to 14 days. If your room temperature is too warm, store them in a sealed container in the refrigerator.

DARK CHOCOLATE TRUFFLES

MAKES: 50 **DIFFICULTY:** ◆ **GLUTEN-FREE**

Chocolate truffles were originally created to replicate the precious black truffle fungus that you find in the ground. They are meant to be irregular in shape and were initially just coated in cocoa powder. A chocolate coating on the outside was eventually added to extend the shelf life. With these truffles, I have kept true to the original concept. They are extremely rich and decadent and make a beautiful centrepiece on the table when serving coffee.

300 g (10½ oz/2 cups) finely chopped
  good-quality dark chocolate
215 ml (7½ fl oz) cream (35% fat)
1 vanilla bean, seeds scraped
25 g (1 oz) liquid glucose
10 g (⅜ oz) unsalted butter
Dutch-process cocoa powder,
  for rolling

Put the chocolate in a bowl. Put the cream, vanilla bean seeds and glucose in a saucepan over medium heat and bring to the boil. Pour the hot mixture over the chocolate, whisking by hand until the chocolate is melted and combined. Add the butter and continue whisking until incorporated. Cover with plastic wrap so it is touching the surface of the ganache. Leave to cool at room temperature (below 23°C/73°F) for 2–3 hours or until the ganache feels firm but pliable when you press on it. If your room temperature is warm, place the ganache in the refrigerator for a short period, just until it firms up enough to pipe.

Sift the cocoa powder onto a sheet of baking paper. Transfer the ganache to a piping (icing) bag with a 1.2 cm (7/16 inch) plain nozzle or just scoop it with a teaspoon directly onto the sifted cocoa powder. Using a teaspoon, gently roll each truffle until it is completely coated in cocoa. Remove the truffles from the tray as you go and they are ready to serve. They are best stored at room temperature in an airtight container for up to 3 days. They are soft, so be gentle when handling them.

CHOCOLATE-DIPPED SQUARES

MAKES: 77   **DIFFICULTY:** ⬛⬛   **GLUTEN-FREE**

The chocolate filling in this recipe is a little different from others as it has a custard base. If you prefer, you can leave out the alcohol or interchange it for another type of liqueur. If you're looking for a more intense flavour, dip the squares in dark chocolate.

GANACHE SQUARES

690 g (1 lb 8 oz) good-quality milk chocolate, coarsely chopped

40 g (1½ oz/about 2) egg yolks

75 g (2¾ oz/⅓ cup) caster (superfine) sugar

250 ml (9 fl oz/1 cup) cream (35% fat)

15 ml (½ fl oz/3 teaspoons) butterscotch schnapps

Line a 33 x 23 cm (13 x 9 inch), or similar sized, baking tin with baking paper so it goes up the sides. Spray a small amount of vegetable oil underneath the paper if needed. Put the chocolate in a heatproof bowl.

Whisk the egg yolks and sugar together by hand in a medium bowl. Put the cream in a saucepan over medium heat and bring to the boil. Pour the hot cream over the egg mixture, whisking by hand to combine. Return the mixture to the pan over low heat, stirring gently with a heatproof flexible spatula or wooden spoon, until the temperature reaches 82°C (180°F), to create an anglaise. (If you don't have a sugar thermometer dip a wooden spoon in the mixture, lift it out and draw a line through the mixture on the spoon with your finger. If the anglaise runs straight over the line, it's not ready. If the line holds without any drips, it's ready. Do this process quickly, before the anglaise runs off the spoon.) Once the anglaise reaches temperature, immediately strain it over the chocolate, whisking by hand until all the chocolate is melted. Whisk in the butterscotch schnapps.

Pour the mixture into the prepared tin and leave at room temperature for a minimum of 24 hours. If your room is too warm (above 23°C/73°F), place the ganache in the refrigerator for a short period of time just until it firms up. Remove your ganache from the tin and mark it with a ruler into individual 3 cm (1¼ inch) squares. Using a large, straight-bladed knife, cut out the squares, cleaning the knife in between each cut. Separate the squares ready for dipping.

800 g (1 lb 12 oz/5⅓ cups) coarsely
    chopped good-quality milk chocolate
Dutch-process cocoa powder, for dusting
acetate, cut into 77 squares of 4 cm
    (1½ inch) (optional)

FINISHING

Temper the chocolate (see pages 12–14). Line a flat tray with baking paper. Pick up one chocolate square at a time, so it's balanced on the end of a dipping fork (use a bamboo skewer if needed to help you balance), and dip it into the chocolate to coat the square with a thin layer of chocolate. Tap the fork a few times on the surface of the chocolate to remove the excess chocolate from the square. Wipe the base of the dipping fork on the side of the bowl and place the chocolate square on your lined tray. Sprinkle the surface with cocoa powder and gently press a square of acetate on top (the plastic square is optional) until it is in direct contact with the chocolate. Keep the plastic square in place for as long as possible to obtain a gloss on the surface of the chocolate.

After every three or four times you use the dipping fork, gently wipe it with paper towel to avoid a build-up of chocolate. Reheat the chocolate as needed with a hair dryer and repeat the process until all the chocolate squares are dipped. Place the squares in the refrigerator for 5–8 minutes, then remove the plastic squares (which can be re-used). The remaining chocolate can be well wrapped and stored in an opaque container until required. These chocolates have a 1-week shelf life. They should be stored in an airtight container at room temperature or in the refrigerator if your room is too warm.

Ganache Discs PAGE 68

GANACHE DISCS

MAKES: 50 DIFFICULTY: ◆ **GLUTEN-FREE**

If you're looking for a rich treat – look no further! If preferred, dip the discs into milk chocolate instead of dark to make them less intense.

175 g (6 oz) good-quality dark chocolate, finely chopped (a)

140 ml (4¾ fl oz) cream (35% fat)

15 g (½ oz/2 teaspoons) liquid glucose

35 g (1¼ oz) unsalted butter, diced

10 ml (¼ fl oz/2 teaspoons) coffee-flavoured cream liqueur, such as Baileys

750 g (1 lb 10 oz/5 cups) coarsely chopped good-quality dark chocolate (b)

Put the chocolate (a) in a heatproof bowl. Put the cream and glucose in a saucepan over medium heat and bring to the boil. Pour the hot cream over the chocolate (a), whisking by hand to combine. Once all the chocolate is fully melted and combined, add the butter, a piece at a time, and continue whisking. Add the liqueur and mix to create a ganache. Scrape the ganache down the side of the bowl and cover with plastic wrap touching the surface of the ganache. Store the ganache at room temperature (23°C/73°F) for a minimum of 5 hours or until it feels firm but pliable when you press on the ganache. If your room temperature is warm, place the ganache in the refrigerator for a short period just until it firms up enough to pipe.

1. Pipe round truffle shapes onto a lined tray.

2. Place a sheet of baking paper on top of the piped ganache.

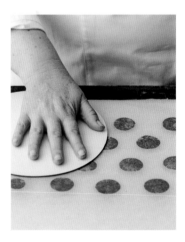

3. Flatten the ganache gently into even discs with some cardboard.

Once the ganache is firm, transfer it to a piping (icing) bag with a 1.2 cm (7/16 inch) plain nozzle and pipe round dollops, approximately 2 cm (¾ inch) in diameter, onto a flat tray lined with baking paper. (You can also use a teaspoon to scoop small amounts onto a lined tray.) Once the tray is full, place another sheet of baking paper on top and press down gently with either another flat tray or a piece of cardboard to create even discs. Be careful not to press too firmly – if the discs are too thin you won't be able to dip them. Leave the discs at room temperature (not above 23°C/73°F) for 3–4 hours. If your room temperature is too warm, you can put the discs in the refrigerator for a short period of time just to firm them up.

Temper the chocolate (b) (see pages 12–14). Line a flat tray with baking paper. Using a fork, place one disc at a time into the tempered chocolate and cover the top of the disc with a thin layer of chocolate. Pick it up so that it sits half off the fork. Tap the fork a few times on the surface of the chocolate to remove the excess. Wipe the base of the dipping fork on the side of the bowl and place the disc onto your prepared tray. With the dipping fork on its side, tap a few times on the surface of the dipped chocolate before it sets, and then pull up and quickly to the side to create a line. After every three to four times you use the dipping fork, gently wipe it with paper towel to avoid a build-up of chocolate. Reheat your chocolate as needed with a hair dryer and repeat the process until all the fillings are dipped. Any remaining chocolate can be well wrapped and stored in an opaque container until required.

CARAMEL CHOCOLATE BARS

MAKES: 33 DIFFICULTY: 🍫🍫

You can, of course, make these chocolate bars without the colourful chocolate dot garnish – but they do make them extra special. If you like, the bars can be cut to create individual chocolates.

BRETON SHORTBREAD

35 g (1¼ oz/⅓ cup) pecans, chopped
75 g (2¾ oz) unsalted butter
65 g (2¼ oz) caster (superfine) sugar
pinch of salt
40 g (1½ oz/about 2) egg yolks
100 g (3½ oz/⅔ cup) plain (all-purpose) flour, plus extra for dusting
10 g (⅜ oz/2 teaspoons) baking powder

Preheat the oven to 160°C (315°F). Put the chopped pecans on a baking tray lined with baking paper and roast them for 10–12 minutes until lightly roasted. Set aside on the tray to cool at room temperature.

Using an electric mixer with a paddle attachment, mix the butter, caster sugar and salt on medium speed until all the butter is smooth. Add the egg yolks, one at a time, mixing well after each addition. Add the flour, baking powder and pecans and mix to combine into a dough. Press the dough into an even, flat square, wrap it in plastic wrap and place it in the refrigerator to rest for 1 hour, or until firm.

Preheat the oven to 170°C (325°F). Line a 28×22 cm (11¼ x 8½ inch) baking tin with baking paper, so the paper goes up the sides of the tin. Lightly dust a work surface with flour and roll the pastry out in an even layer to fit the baking tin snugly. Bake for approximately 12–15 minutes until golden brown. Leave in the tin to cool at room temperature.

CARAMEL

560 ml (19¼ fl oz/2¼ cups) cream (35% fat)
430 g (15¼ oz) caster (superfine) sugar
150 g (5½ oz) liquid glucose
290 g (10¼ oz) unsalted butter
60 g (2¼ oz/2 tablespoons) honey
pinch of salt
½ teaspoon bicarbonate of soda (baking soda)

Put the cream in a saucepan over medium heat and bring to the boil. Put the sugar, glucose and 85 ml (2¾ fl oz) water in a large saucepan over medium heat and heat until the temperature reaches 145°C (293°F). (If you haven't got a sugar thermometer, when the sugar reaches temperature it should still be clear and when a small amount of sugar is dropped into iced water it should be firm to the touch.) Once you reach temperature, whisk in the butter, honey and then the hot liquid cream. To prevent the temperature of the sugar from dropping below 110°C (230°F), pour in the cream in two or three stages, whisking as you go. Add the salt and bicarbonate of soda and continue whisking until the temperature reaches 119°C (246°F). (If you don't have a sugar thermometer, drop a small amount into some iced water and it should have a firm but slightly pliable consistency.) Pour the caramel on top of the prepared Breton shortbread in the tin. Leave at room temperature for 2 hours for the caramel to set. 👉

Once set, remove the caramel shortbread from the tin, remove the baking paper and place the shortbread on a chopping board. Oil a large, straight-bladed knife and measure out and mark the caramel into 8 x 2 cm (3¼ x ¾ inch) bars. Using the oiled knife, cut each bar, cleaning and re-oiling the knife as needed. Separate the bars and dip them the same day they are made, so the caramel doesn't go too soft (see opposite).

GARNISH

oil-based powdered food colouring
250 g (9 oz) good-quality white chocolate, coarsely chopped

You can choose any oil-based colours that you like to garnish the chocolate bars or simply leave the chocolate white. I recommend that you make one colour at a time. You can make yellow and then add other colours and turn it into orange/red/purple etc., rather than making all the colours at once.

Temper the chocolate (see pages 12–14). Sift in small amounts of the colour into the chocolate, stir and add more colour as needed. Place the prepared coloured chocolate in a paper piping (icing) cone (see page 19) or a zip-lock bag and cut a small amount off the tip of the cone or off the bottom corner of the zip-lock bag with scissors. Pipe dots of various sizes, 2–10 mm (1/16–½ inch), onto a sheet of baking paper and repeat the process with each colour until you have a variety of sizes in different colours. You will need about five dots for each bar. Leave the dots at room temperature to set or, if your room temperature exceeds 23°C (73°F), set them in the refrigerator for 5 minutes. These can be made months in advance and stored in an airtight container.

1. *Pipe the coloured dots for garnishing.*

1.2 kg (2 lb 10 oz/8 cups) coarsely chopped good-quality milk chocolate

Temper the chocolate (see pages 12–14). Line a tray with baking paper. Pick up one caramel bar at a time, so it sits in the centre of the dipping fork (use a bamboo skewer if needed to help you balance it), dip it in the chocolate and coat the bar with a thin layer of chocolate. Tap the fork a few times on the surface of the chocolate to remove the excess chocolate. Wipe the base of the dipping fork on the side of the bowl and place the chocolate bar on the lined tray. Place the prepared chocolate dots on the top of the bar before the milk chocolate sets. After every three or four times you use the dipping fork, gently wipe it with some paper towel to avoid a build-up of chocolate. Reheat the chocolate as needed with a hair dryer and repeat the process until all the chocolate bars are dipped. The remaining chocolate can be well wrapped and stored in an opaque container until required. These chocolate bars will store in an airtight container at room temperature for up to 3 weeks.

2. *Press the chocolate bar into the milk chocolate.*

3. *Pull it out with a dipping fork and remove the excess chocolate from the base.*

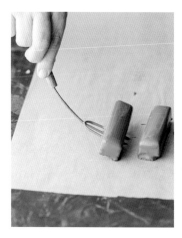

4. *Place the dipped chocolate bars onto a lined tray.*

MOULDED CHOCOLATES

MAKES: 50 **DIFFICULTY:** 🍫🍫🍫 **GLUTEN-FREE**

Moulded chocolates look like sparkling jewels — the plastic mould makes the chocolate contract and become shiny. Handle the chocolates as little as possible to maintain the shine. You can make these moulded chocolates with milk or dark chocolate if you prefer.

100 g (3½ oz) good-quality white
   chocolate, coarsely chopped (a)
red oil-based powdered food colouring
500 g (1 lb 2 oz) good-quality white
   chocolate, coarsely chopped (b)

CHOCOLATE SHELLS

Temper the chocolate (a) (see pages 12–14). Sift in the red food colouring and mix to combine. Polish chocolate moulds with cotton wool to eliminate any fingerprints. (I have used two heart-shaped moulds for this recipe. All moulds vary in shape and size – select ones you like.) Using your finger or a brush, paint a thin layer of the red chocolate into the base of each mould and scrape the top of the mould with a metal scraper to remove any excess red chocolate from the top surface of the mould.

Temper the chocolate (b) (see pages 12–14).

Once the first red chocolate layer has set, fill the mould with the tempered white chocolate and scrape the top and sides of the mould to remove any excess chocolate. Tap or vibrate the mould on a work surface from side to side to dislodge any air bubbles trapped on the surface. Turn the mould upside down suspended above a sheet of baking paper and tap it firmly on the side of the mould with a scraper or palette knife to remove the excess chocolate. (Once set, the chocolate on the baking paper can be stored and re-tempered for 'Sealing the mould' – see page 77.) Scrape the mould while still upside down to remove any drips of chocolate. Turn the mould the right way up and tap and scrape again if necessary. Place the mould on its side to set or if your room temperature is warm, place for a short period in the refrigerator. ☞

GANACHE FILLING

200 g (7 oz/1⅓ cups) coarsely chopped
good-quality milk chocolate
100 g (3½ oz/⅔ cup) coarsely chopped
good-quality dark chocolate
260 ml (9 fl oz) cream (35% fat)
1 vanilla bean, seeds scraped
1 teaspoon unsalted butter

Put both chocolates in a heatproof bowl. Put the cream and vanilla bean seeds in a saucepan over medium heat and bring to the boil. Pour the hot cream over the chocolate, whisking by hand until all the chocolate is melted and combined. Add the butter, whisking to combine. Scrape the ganache down from the side of the bowl and cover with plastic wrap so it is touching the surface of the ganache. Leave the ganache until it cools to just below 30°C (86°F), then use immediately.

Transfer the prepared ganache to a piping (icing) bag with a 5–10 mm (¼–½ inch) plain nozzle. Pipe the ganache into each chocolate-lined mould, leaving space to seal the mould with more chocolate. (You can also use a teaspoon to spoon the ganache into the moulds.) Leave to cool at room temperature – as long as the temperature doesn't exceed 23°C (73°F). If the room is too hot, place the ganache in an airtight container in the refrigerator for 1 hour or up to 24 hours before sealing, to enable the ganache to firm up. You can also put the mould in the refrigerator, but for no longer than 15 minutes.

1. Place a thin layer of red chocolate onto the surface of the mould.

2. Fill the mould with the prepared white chocolate.

3. Scrape off the excess chocolate.

4. *Turn the mould over and tap out any excess chocolate onto a sheet of baking paper.*

5. *Scrape the top of the mould clean.*

6. *Pipe in the ganache.*

SEALING THE MOULD

Once the ganache has been setting for a minimum of 1 hour in the mould, temper the remaining white chocolate (see pages 12–14) that was tapped out of the mould. If your mould has been sitting for more than 12 hours, warm the surface slightly with a hair dryer. Place a sheet of baking paper under the mould. Spread a layer of tempered chocolate on the base of the mould and tap on the side of the mould with the handle of a palette knife or spatula to pop any air bubbles. Scrape firmly on the surface of the mould with a metal scraper wider than the mould or a metal spatula. Scrape again if needed and then scrape the excess chocolate off the sides of the mould and repeat the process with the second mould.

Let the moulds sit at room temperature for 10 minutes and then place in the refrigerator for 20 minutes. Turn the mould over onto a clean work surface and tap to dislodge the chocolates. As soon as they come out, move them gently to the side and tap again if needed. Store the chocolates at room temperature – as long as the temperature doesn't exceed 23°C (73°F). If the room is too hot, store them in an airtight container in the refrigerator for up to a week.

ORANGE & HAZELNUT CHOCOLATE BARS

MAKES: 44 DIFFICULTY: 🍫🍫🍫

If you prefer, these decadent creations can be made as bars or as individual chocolates. If you're after a more intense chocolate flavour, dip these into dark chocolate instead of milk.

HAZELNUT PASTRY

115 g (4 oz) unsalted butter

1 vanilla bean, seeds scraped, or
  ½ teaspoon vanilla bean paste

85 g (3 oz) caster (superfine) sugar

80 g (2¾ oz/about 1½) whole eggs

½ teaspoon ground cinnamon

pinch of salt

½ teaspoon ground cardamom

50 g (1¾ oz) hazelnut meal

220 g (7¾ oz) plain (all-purpose) flour,
  plus extra for dusting

1 teaspoon baking powder

Line a 33 x 23 cm (13 x 9 inch), or similar sized, baking tin with baking paper so it goes up the sides. Spray a small amount of vegetable oil underneath the paper if needed.

Using an electric mixer with a paddle attachment, mix the butter, vanilla bean seeds or paste and sugar on medium speed until the butter is fully incorporated. Add the eggs, one at a time, mixing well after each addition. Add the remaining ingredients and mix until combined. Press the dough into an even, flat square, wrap it in plastic wrap and place it in the refrigerator to rest for 1 hour, or until firm.

Preheat the oven to 170°C (325°F). Lightly dust a work surface with flour before rolling the pastry out to a 4 mm (3/16 inch) thickness, just to fit the tray. Trim the pastry to fit flat on the base of the prepared tin. Bake for 10–12 minutes until golden brown. Leave to cool in the tin at room temperature. ☞

GANACHE FILLING

100 g (3½ oz/⅔ cup) finely chopped
  good-quality milk chocolate
290 g (10¼ oz) good-quality dark
  chocolate, finely chopped
250 ml (9 fl oz/1 cup) cream (35% fat)
zest of 1 orange
10 g (⅜ oz) unsalted butter

Put the two chocolates in a heatproof bowl. Put the cream and orange zest in a saucepan over medium heat and bring to the boil. Remove the pan from the heat, cover the pan and leave to infuse for 15 minutes. Return the mixture to the heat and bring to the boil again, then pour the hot cream over the chocolate. Whisk together by hand until the chocolate is melted and completely combined. Whisk in the butter. Pour the mixture directly over the cooled hazelnut base in the tin and leave overnight at room temperature. If your room temperature is too warm, place the chocolate-covered base in the refrigerator for a short period of time to firm up after it has sat overnight.

Remove your ganache-topped base from the tin and mark it with a ruler into individual 8 x 2 cm (3¼ x ¾ inch) bars. Using a large, straight-bladed knife, cut the rectangles, cleaning your knife in between each cut. Separate the bars ready for dipping.

ORANGE ZEST GARNISH

1 orange
150 g (5½ oz/⅔ cup) caster (superfine)
  sugar, plus extra for rolling

Preheat the oven to 50°C (120°F). Zest the orange with a peeler to create long strips of orange zest.

Put the sugar and 100 ml (3½ fl oz) water in a saucepan over medium heat and boil until the sugar is dissolved. Submerge the orange peel in the syrup and bring to the boil again. Strain the orange zest and discard the remaining syrup.

Spread the extra caster sugar out on a tray lined with baking paper and roll the zest in the sugar until well coated. Bake in the oven for 45 minutes or until completely dry. Store in an airtight container at room temperature for up to 2 weeks.

1. *Zest the orange to prepare the garnish.*

2. *Place the prepared chocolate bar into the milk chocolate.*

1.2 kg (2 lb 10 oz/8 cups) coarsely
chopped good-quality milk chocolate

Temper the chocolate (see pages 12–14). Line a flat tray with baking paper.
Pick up one bar at a time, so it sits in the centre of a dipping fork (use a bamboo
skewer if needed to help you balance it) and dip it in the chocolate to coat the
bar with a thin layer of chocolate. Tap the fork gently a few times on the surface
of the chocolate to remove the excess chocolate from the bar. Wipe the base of
the dipping fork on the side of the bowl and place the chocolate bar on your
lined tray. Place the prepared orange zest garnish on the top of the bar before
the milk chocolate sets. After every three or four times you use the dipping
fork, gently wipe it with paper towel to avoid a build-up of chocolate. Reheat
the chocolate as needed with a hair dryer and repeat the process until all the
chocolate bars are dipped. The remaining chocolate can be well wrapped and
stored in an opaque container until required. These chocolate bars have a
3-week shelf life.

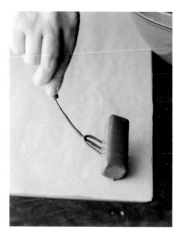

3. *Place it on a dipping fork to remove it and drain off the excess chocolate.*

4. *Place the chocolate bar onto a lined tray.*

3.
BAKED

BROWNIES

MAKES: 32 DIFFICULTY:

A big call, but I would have to say that this is the best chocolate brownie that I've tasted. To create a beautiful flavour, it's important that you use the best quality chocolate you can source.

115 g (4 oz) unsalted butter

230 g (8 oz) good-quality dark chocolate (a)

100 g (3½ oz) caster (superfine) sugar

100 g (3½ oz/½ cup lightly packed) soft brown sugar

180 g (6½ oz/about 3) whole eggs

½ teaspoon vanilla bean paste

80 g (2¾ oz) plain (all-purpose) flour

¼ teaspoon baking powder

15 g (½ oz) Dutch-process cocoa powder

pinch of salt

90 g (3¼ oz) good-quality milk chocolate chips

90 g (3¼ oz) good-quality dark chocolate chips (b)

Preheat the oven to 170°C (325°F). Grease the inside of two 16 cm (6¼ inch) square cake tins with oil spray before lining the bases and sides with baking paper.

Melt the butter and dark chocolate (a) together in a double boiler or in a plastic bowl in the microwave (see page 12). In a mixing bowl, combine the two sugars, the eggs and vanilla bean paste and whisk by hand to combine. Add the butter and chocolate mix then sift the dry ingredients and fold them through the mixture to gently combine.

Finely chop the milk and dark chocolate chips (b) and add them to the brownie mixture. Divide the mixture evenly between the prepared tins and bake for approximately 25 minutes, or until crusty on top and soft in the centre. Leave to cool in the tins, then turn out onto a wire rack.

Once cool, cut into 4 cm (1½ inch) squares. These brownies are perfect to eat on their own, or you can eat them warm with a scoop of vanilla ice cream and a drizzle of salted caramel for a dessert. They freeze well for up to a month when well wrapped in plastic wrap.

LAMINGTONS

MAKES: 9 DIFFICULTY: ◼ **GLUTEN-FREE**

The lamington is an Australian classic – and here, I've added a more chocolaty twist. These are so moist and delicious it is difficult to resist going back for seconds.

100 g (3½ oz/about 5) egg yolks
120 g (4¼ oz) caster (superfine) sugar
125 g (4½ oz/about 5) egg whites
pinch of cream of tartar
20 g (¾ oz) Dutch-process cocoa powder
50 g (1¾ oz) cornflour (cornstarch)
65 g (2¼ oz) good-quality dark chocolate, coarsely chopped

FLOURLESS CHOCOLATE SPONGE

Preheat the oven to 165°C (320°F). Grease the inside of a 16 cm (6¼ inch) square cake tin with oil spray before lining the base and sides with baking paper. Using an electric mixer with a whisk attachment, beat the egg yolks and half the sugar on high speed until pale. In a separate clean bowl, whisk the egg whites and cream of tartar on medium–high speed until medium peaks form. Gradually add the remaining caster sugar. Continue mixing for 1 minute, then remove the whisk attachment.

Sift the cocoa powder and cornflour together. Melt the dark chocolate in a double boiler or in a plastic bowl in the microwave (see page 12). Fold the sifted ingredients and melted chocolate through the whipped egg yolk mixture with a spatula, then gently fold this mixture into the whisked egg whites. Pour the finished sponge mixture into the prepared tin and bake for 30–35 minutes. The sponge is ready when you gently press the centre of the cake and it bounces back. Remove from the oven and cool at room temperature before wrapping in plastic wrap and placing in the freezer. (At this stage the sponge can be stored in the freezer for a few weeks prior to using. Ensure that it is well wrapped before freezing.) ☞

RASPBERRY JAM

140 g (5 oz) frozen raspberries
115 g (4 oz) caster (superfine) sugar
30 g (1 oz/1 tablespoon) liquid glucose

Put the raspberries, sugar and glucose in a saucepan over medium heat and bring to the boil, stirring. Continue to heat until it reaches a temperature of 103°C (217°F), or test until you achieve a soft jam consistency. (Placing a small amount on a chilled plate will give you an idea of what the consistency will be like once set.) Remove the jam from the heat, transfer it to a bowl and cover with plastic wrap directly touching the surface of the jam.

CHOCOLATE SOAKING SYRUP

240 g (8½ oz) caster (superfine) sugar
90 g (3¼ oz) Dutch-process cocoa powder
40 g (1½ oz) raspberry jam (see recipe above – or you can use store-bought jam if you are short on time)

Put the sugar, 240 ml (8 fl oz) water, the cocoa powder and raspberry jam in a saucepan over medium heat and stir until the sugar is dissolved. Mix together with a whisk or a hand-held blender until combined. Set aside to cool. (The chocolate soaking syrup can be made up to 4 days in advance and stored in the refrigerator or freezer.)

COCONUT COATING

180 g (6½ oz/2 cups) desiccated (shredded) coconut
25 g (1 oz) Dutch-process cocoa powder

Put the desiccated coconut and cocoa powder in a bowl and rub them together by hand to combine.

ASSEMBLY

Remove the sponge from the freezer and trim the top with a serrated knife to get a flat surface. While still frozen, cut the sponge into nine equal portions.

Using the handle of a teaspoon, create a hole in the centre of each sponge by removing a small amount of sponge but not going through to the base. Either using a spoon or a piping (icing) bag with a small plain nozzle, place the prepared jam into the hole, filling it to the top.

Dip each filled sponge individually into the prepared chocolate soaking syrup by hand to cover all sides. Transfer immediately to the bowl of coconut coating, and cover all sides of the lamingtons. These lamingtons are best stored at room temperature in an airtight container for up to 2 days.

1. Take a small amount out of the centre of each sponge with a teaspoon.

2. Fill each centre with jam.

3. Dip each sponge into the chocolate syrup to coat.

4. Coat each sponge in the coconut coating.

CHOCOLATE CUPCAKES

MAKES: 12 **DIFFICULTY:** ◆

The chocolate ganache topping is a divine finish on top of these cupcakes;
it can be coated on with a knife or piped in a elegant pattern.

CHOCOLATE CUPCAKES

20 ml (¾ fl oz/1 tablespoon) espresso
  coffee or strong coffee
65 g (2¼ oz) Dutch-process cocoa powder
225 g (8 oz/1½ cups) self-raising flour
pinch of bicarbonate of soda
  (baking soda)
pinch of salt
115 g (4 oz) caster (superfine) sugar
115 g (4 oz) soft brown sugar
120 g (4¼ oz/about 2) whole eggs
115 g (4 oz) unsalted butter, melted
140 g (5 oz) sour cream
50 ml (1¾ fl oz) vegetable oil
175 g (6 oz) good-quality milk chocolate,
  coarsely chopped
6 marshmallows
70 g (2½ oz/¼ cup) crunchy peanut butter
12 chewy caramels

Preheat the oven to 170°C (325°F). Put the coffee, 20 ml (¾ fl oz/1 tablespoon) water and the cocoa powder in a bowl and stir to create a paste.

Put the flour, bicarbonate of soda, salt and sugars in the bowl of an electric mixer with a paddle attachment and mix on medium speed until combined. Add the eggs one at a time, beating well after each addition, followed by the coffee paste, melted butter, sour cream, vegetable oil and chopped milk chocolate.

Place 12 paper cases in a cupcake tin (or line the holes with baking paper). Cut the marshmallows in half and place a piece in each paper case. Place a small portion of peanut butter on top of each piece of marshmallow. Cut the chewy caramels into four pieces and place on top of the peanut butter in each paper case.

Evenly divide the chocolate cupcake batter into the cases on top of the fillings. Bake for 15–20 minutes. The cupcakes are ready when you gently tap the centre of the cake and it bounces back. Remove the cupcakes from the oven and leave to cool in the tin for 10 minutes, before removing them and transferring to a wire rack to cool completely.

CHOCOLATE GANACHE TOPPING

250 g (9 oz/1⅔ cups) finely chopped
  good-quality milk chocolate
120 ml (4 fl oz) cream (35% fat)

Put the chocolate in a heatproof bowl. Put the cream in a saucepan over medium heat and bring to the boil. Pour the hot cream over the chocolate, whisking until combined. Put a piece of plastic wrap directly on the surface of the ganache and leave to set at room temperature for approximately 2 hours until it reaches a piping consistency.

Once the ganache has set, put it in a piping (icing) bag with a 1 cm (½ inch) star-shaped nozzle and pipe one swirl on top of each cupcake. (Alternatively, you can just spoon or spread the ganache on the cakes.) These cupcakes can keep for up to 4 days in an airtight container at room temperature.

BERRY MERINGUE CAKE

SERVES: 8-10 DIFFICULTY: ◆

*You can't go wrong with this quick and easy cake, which can be made
gluten-free by replacing the flour with a good-quality gluten-free flour.*

CHOCOLATE DACQUOISE

225 g (8 oz/about 9) egg whites
pinch of cream of tartar
130 g (4½ oz) caster (superfine) sugar
80 g (2¾ oz/¾ cup) almond meal
80 g (2¾ oz/¾ cup) hazelnut meal
125 g (4½ oz/1 cup) icing (confectioners')
  sugar
40 g (1½ oz) plain (all-purpose) flour
40 g (1½ oz/⅓ cup) Dutch-process
  cocoa powder

Preheat the oven to 170°C (325°F). Prepare an 18 cm (7 inch), 4.5 cm (1¾ inch) high cake ring or tin (see page 16).

Using an electric mixer with a whisk attachment, beat the egg whites and cream of tartar on high speed until medium peaks form. Gradually add the caster sugar and continue whisking for 1 minute, or until the sugar is dissolved. Fold through the sifted remaining ingredients using a spatula until well combined.

BERRY COMPOTE

50 g (1¾ oz/⅓ cup) strawberries,
  coarsely chopped
100 g (3½ oz) frozen raspberries
40 g (1½ oz/¼ cup) blueberries
½ teaspoon vanilla bean paste
40 g (1½ oz) caster (superfine) sugar

Put all the ingredients in a saucepan over medium heat and bring to a simmer. Cook for 2 minutes, stirring gently, then remove from the heat and set aside. Allow to cool before using.

Transfer the chocolate dacquoise to a piping (icing) bag fitted with a 1.2 cm (7/16 inch) plain nozzle. Pipe (or spoon) half the mixture into the prepared cake tin to come 2 cm (¾ inch) up the side. Pour the prepared berry compote onto the centre of the dacquoise mixture, spreading it evenly to about 1 cm (½ inch) from the side of the tin.

Pipe the remaining dacquoise on top of the compote until around 3 cm (1¼ inches) high. Alternatively, spread the remaining dacquoise roughly over the compote, creating peaks with a spatula. Bake for 35–40 minutes until golden with a firm crust. Cool before turning out and removing the ring.

This cake is best stored in an airtight container at room temperature for 2–3 days. Alternatively, freeze in an airtight container for 3–4 weeks. If freezing, defrost in the refrigerator overnight and serve at room temperature.

RUM & RAISIN CHOCOLATE CAKE

SERVES: 12 DIFFICULTY: ◼

A classic flavour combination, this moist and rich chocolate cake is more suited to adult tastes. If you prefer, omit the rum but still soak the raisins in water to make it more child friendly.

215 g (7½ oz/1¼ cups) raisins
boiling water
150 ml (5 fl oz) light white rum
195 g (7 oz) unsalted butter
135 g (4¾ oz) soft brown sugar
pinch of salt
220 g (7¾ oz) good-quality dark
  chocolate, coarsely chopped
300 g (10½ oz/about 5) whole eggs
260 g (9¼ oz/1¾ cups) self-raising flour

RUM & RAISIN CAKE

Preheat the oven to 165°C (320°F). Chop the raisins roughly, put them in a bowl and cover with boiling water to rehydrate. Soak for 5 minutes before draining. Pour the rum over the raisins and immediately seal the bowl tightly with plastic wrap. (Heating the raisins with the boiling water will enable them to absorb the rum faster.)

Using an electric mixer with a paddle attachment, mix the butter, sugar and salt on medium speed until light and creamy.

Melt the chocolate in a double boiler or in a plastic bowl in the microwave (see page 12). Add it to the whipped butter and sugar in the electric mixer bowl and beat until the chocolate is combined, scraping the side of the bowl down as needed.

Put the eggs in a bowl over a saucepan of simmering water (ensuring the bowl doesn't touch the water) and heat the mixture to body temperature while whisking (this helps to stop the cake batter splitting). Gradually add the egg to the chocolate mixture, ensuring that each addition is fully incorporated before adding more, scraping down the side of the bowl as needed. Once the egg is fully combined, add the self-raising flour and stop mixing once combined.

Drain the raisins, reserving the rum, and set aside several rum-soaked raisins for garnish. Add the rum to the cake mixture, followed by the raisins and fold into the cake batter using a spatula.

Spray a 22 x 10 cm (8½ x 4 inch) loaf (bar) tin with vegetable oil and line it with baking paper. Pour the cake mixture into the tin and bake for 45 minutes, or until a metal skewer inserted in the cake comes out clean. Leave to cool in the tin at room temperature for 10 minutes before transferring to a wire rack to cool completely.

CHOCOLATE TOPPING

125 g (4½ oz) good-quality milk
  chocolate, coarsely chopped
40 g (1½ oz) honey
75 ml (2½ fl oz) cream (35% fat)

Put the chocolate in a heatproof bowl. Put the honey and cream in a saucepan over medium heat and bring to the boil. Pour the hot mixture over the chocolate, whisking by hand until combined and shiny.

FINISHING

edible gold metallic or lustre powder
small block of dark chocolate, coarsely
  chopped
rum-soaked raisins (reserved,
  see opposite)

Once the cake has cooled completely, remove the baking paper and spread the chocolate topping on the top surface of the cake. Sprinkle with a small amount of edible gold powder. Garnish down the centre of the iced cake with chopped dark chocolate and a few rum-soaked raisins. A thin slice of this cake is perfect for afternoon tea or warmed served with ice cream as a dessert. Keep in an airtight container at room temperature for up to 5 days.

Rum & Raisin Chocolate Cake PAGE 94

CHOCOLATE DATE MERINGUE CAKE

SERVES: 20 DIFFICULTY: 🔲 **GLUTEN-FREE**

If you're looking to cater for a large crowd of chocolate lovers, look no further. If eaten as soon as it's assembled, you can appreciate the contrast of crunchy meringue to soft mousse. Once stored, it's equally delicious and easier to cut as the chocolate mousse seeps into the meringue.

CHOCOLATE DATE MERINGUE DISCS

150 g (5½ oz/about 6) egg whites

½ teaspoon cream of tartar

200 g (7 oz) caster (superfine) sugar

200 g (7 oz/2 cups) pecans, coarsely chopped

200 g (7 oz) pitted dates, coarsely chopped into 1 cm (½ inch) pieces

150 g (5½ oz/1 cup) coarsely chopped good-quality dark chocolate

50 g (1¾ oz/⅓ cup) coarsely chopped good-quality milk chocolate

Preheat the oven to 160°C (315°F). Line two large baking trays with baking paper.

Using an electric mixer with a whisk attachment, whip the egg whites with the cream of tartar on medium–high speed until medium peaks form, then gradually add the sugar. Continue to whisk for a minute to dissolve the sugar. Fold the chopped pecans, dates and chocolate through the meringue using a spatula.

Divide the meringue mixture into four equal portions then spread the meringue on the baking trays into four individual discs, approximately 23 cm (9 inches) in diameter. Bake for approximately 15 minutes, until lightly coloured. Cool at room temperature. (The meringue discs can be pre-made and stored for a week prior to assembly if well wrapped.)

MILK CHOCOLATE MOUSSE FILLING

650 g (1 lb 7 oz/4⅓ cups) coarsely chopped good-quality milk chocolate

510 ml (17 fl oz) cream (35% fat) (a)

½ teaspoon vanilla bean paste

400 ml (14 fl oz) cream (35% fat) (b)

Put the chocolate in a heatproof bowl. Put the cream (a) and the vanilla bean paste in a saucepan over medium heat and bring to the boil. Pour the hot cream over the chocolate and whisk until the chocolate melts and you have created a smooth ganache. Allow to cool to touch, but not so far that it sets.

Whisk the cream (b) to a semi-whipped consistency (see page 16) and fold it through the ganache until combined.

GARNISH

50 g (1¾ oz/½ cup) pecans
100 g (3½ oz/⅔ cup) coarsely chopped
  good-quality dark chocolate

Preheat the oven to 150°C (300°F). Put the pecans on a baking tray lined with baking paper and roast them for approximately 15 minutes. Remove them from the oven and, once cool, cut them into large chunks.

Temper the chocolate (see pages 12–14). Cut 30 x 10 cm (12 x 4 inch) rectangles of baking paper and either pipe with a paper piping (icing) cone (see page 19), or spoon on a 1.5 cm (⅝ inch) dot of tempered chocolate, and smear it into a curved shape with your thumbs. Repeat this process to create chocolate garnishes for the top of the cake. Leave the garnishes at room temperature to set for approximately 20 minutes. If your room temperature is too warm (more than 23°C/73°F), place them in the refrigerator for no more than 5 minutes.

ASSEMBLY

icing (confectioners') sugar, for dusting

Place one of the meringue discs on your chosen plate, then take a quarter of the prepared milk chocolate mousse filling and spread it evenly over the meringue disc using a palette knife. Layer with a second meringue disc and repeat the process until all the meringue discs are layered with the milk chocolate mousse filling. Place the remaining mousse filling on top of the fourth disc.

Place the curved chocolate garnishes, standing upright, on top of the cake with the widest point on the base. Randomly place the garnishes on the top surface of the mousse and scatter the pecans over. Dust with icing sugar just prior to serving. This cake can be stored in an airtight container in the refrigerator for up to 2 days.

RHUBARB & CHOCOLATE BAKE WITH CRUMBLE TOP

SERVES: 12-14 DIFFICULTY: ◆

I love the flavour of rhubarb – the tartness balances well with the sweetness of chocolate. If preferred, replace the rhubarb with stone fruits.

180 g (6½ oz) unsalted butter
195 g (7 oz) caster (superfine) sugar
pinch of salt
300 g (10½ oz/about 5) whole eggs
80 ml (2½ fl oz/⅓ cup) vegetable oil
280 g (10 oz) plain (all-purpose) flour, sifted
pinch of baking powder, sifted
105 g (3¾ oz) white chocolate, finely chopped

350 g (12 oz) rhubarb, peeled and roughly chopped
140 g (5 oz) caster (superfine) sugar
½ teaspoon vanilla bean paste
1 cinnamon stick

95 g (3¼ oz) unsalted butter
50 g (1¾ oz) soft brown sugar
¾ teaspoon ground cinnamon
95 g (3¼ oz) plain (all-purpose) flour

WHITE CHOCOLATE CAKE

Using an electric mixer with a paddle attachment, beat the butter, sugar and salt until light and creamy. Put the eggs in a bowl over a saucepan of simmering water (ensuring the bowl doesn't touch the water) and heat the mixture to body temperature while whisking (this helps to stop the cake batter splitting). Gradually add the egg to the butter mixture, mixing well before adding more. Slowly add the vegetable oil in a constant drizzle. Remove the bowl from the mixer and gently fold through the sifted flour and baking powder using a spatula. Finally, add the chopped chocolate and combine.

RHUBARB CENTRE

Put the rhubarb, sugar, vanilla bean paste and cinnamon stick in a frying pan over low heat and sauté until the rhubarb is tender. Set aside.

CRUMBLE

Using an electric mixer with a paddle attachment, mix the butter on medium speed until softened. Add the sugar and cinnamon and continue mixing until a smooth paste forms. Add the flour and mix until it just starts coming together as a crumble.

ASSEMBLY

Preheat the oven to 170°C (325°F). Prepare a 22 cm (8½ inch) cake ring or tin (see page 16). Half-fill the cake ring with the cake mixture and then place half the rhubarb pieces on top. Top with the remaining cake mixture. Scatter over the remaining rhubarb then cover with the prepared crumble. Bake for 50–65 minutes. Insert a metal skewer into the centre of the cake and it should come out clean when the cake is ready. This cake is best served at room temperature. It can be stored in an airtight container in the freezer for up to 3 weeks.

DECADENT CHOCOLATE CAKE

SERVES: 12-14 DIFFICULTY: 🍫 **GLUTEN-FREE**

Simple and luscious, this rich cake is perfect served as an afternoon tea or as a dessert with some fresh berries and drizzled cream.

CHOCOLATE CAKE

260 g (9¼ oz) almond meal

115 g (4 oz) icing (confectioners') sugar

120 g (4¼ oz) caster (superfine) sugar

120 g (4¼ oz/about 2) whole eggs

320 g (11¼ oz/about 16) egg yolks

100 ml (3½ fl oz) vegetable oil

pinch of salt

80 g (2¾ oz/¾ cup) Dutch-process cocoa powder, sifted

pinch of baking powder, sifted

140 g (5 oz) unsalted butter

180 g (6½ oz) good-quality dark chocolate, coarsely chopped

Preheat the oven to 160°C (315°F). Prepare a 22 cm (8½ inch) cake ring or tin (see page 16). Put the almond meal and both sugars in the bowl of an electric mixer with a paddle attachment and beat well on low speed to combine. Gradually add the whole eggs and egg yolks, mixing well after each addition. Slowly add the vegetable oil in a constant drizzle, followed by the salt, regularly scraping down the side of the bowl. Using a spatula, gently fold in the sifted cocoa powder and baking powder until just combined.

Melt the butter and chocolate together in a double boiler or in a plastic bowl in the microwave (see page 12). Add the butter and chocolate mixture to the cake batter and mix together using a spatula until well combined. Pour the mixture into the prepared cake tin and hollow out the centre slightly (about 1 cm/½ inch deep) with a spoon. Bake for 50–55 minutes. To test if it is ready, insert a metal skewer or small knife in the centre of the cake – it should come out a little bit sticky just in the centre.

CHOCOLATE GANACHE TOPPING

110 g (3¾ oz/¾ cup) coarsely chopped good-quality dark chocolate

80 ml (2½ fl oz/⅓ cup) cream (35% fat)

10 ml (¼ fl oz/2 teaspoons) orange liqueur (optional)

Put the chocolate in a heatproof bowl. Put the cream in a saucepan over medium heat and bring to the boil. Pour the hot cream over the chocolate, whisking by hand until combined and the chocolate is melted. Add the orange liqueur and continue whisking until combined.

small block of milk chocolate
lavender flowers

GARNISH

Using a large knife or vegetable peeler, scrape chocolate shavings from the chocolate block and set aside. Pick the very centre of each lavender flower for decorating.

ASSEMBLY

Remove the cake from the tin once cool and peel off the baking paper. Spread the chocolate ganache on top with a palette knife. Place the individual chocolate shavings around the edge of the top of the cake and place the lavender flowers around the shavings. This cake can be stored covered in plastic wrap at room temperature for up to 5 days.

Decadent Chocolate Cake PAGE 102

CHOCOLATE CHEESECAKE

SERVES: 10-12 DIFFICULTY: 🍫 **GLUTEN-FREE**

You'll find it difficult to stop at just one slice of this beautiful chocolate cheesecake, which is best served cold. The chocolate bark on top is a great accompaniment, creating a nice snap that contrasts with the creamy cheesecake texture.

CHEESECAKE BASE

170 g (6 oz) chocolate biscuits (cookies) with no filling (gluten-free if required)
70 g (2½ oz) unsalted butter, melted

Crush the biscuits to create a rough crumb. Combine the melted butter with the crushed biscuits and press the mixture into the base of a baking paper–lined 22 cm (8½ inch) cake ring or springform cake tin. Put the cheesecake base into the refrigerator for approximately 15 minutes to set.

CHEESECAKE

170 g (6 oz) good-quality milk chocolate, coarsely chopped
580 g (1 lb 4 oz/2½ cups) cream cheese
210 g (7½ oz) caster (superfine) sugar
1 teaspoon vanilla bean paste
zest of 3 oranges
180 g (6½ oz/about 3) whole eggs
170 g (6 oz) frozen raspberries

Preheat the oven to 150°C (300°F). Melt the chocolate in a double boiler or in a plastic bowl in the microwave (see page 12). Using an electric mixer with a paddle attachment, mix the cream cheese on medium speed until softened. Add the sugar, vanilla bean paste and orange zest and mix to combine. Slowly add the eggs, scraping the bowl down as you go, to ensure they are mixed in evenly. Add the frozen raspberries and gently fold them through the cheesecake mixture.

Spoon the prepared cheesecake mixture on top of the biscuit base and bake for approximately 50 minutes. Tap the top surface of the cheesecake to check if it is baked enough — it should have a slight movement but feel firm. It will rise up as it bakes and drop back down once it cools. Leave to cool at room temperature.

1. Press the cheesecake base into the lined cake tin.

2. Spread the chocolate onto a strip of plastic or baking paper.

3. Place a strip of baking paper on top and roll it up.

4. Once set, unroll it to create your chocolate garnishes.

FINISHING

150 g (5½ oz/1 cup) coarsely chopped good-quality dark chocolate
Dutch-process cocoa powder, for dusting

Cut a 35 x 15 cm (14 x 6 inch) piece of baking paper or plastic. Temper the chocolate (see pages 12–14). Spread a thin layer of the chocolate onto the strip of baking paper with a palette knife and gently roll it into a tube approximately 2 cm (¾ inch) in diameter. Place in the refrigerator to set for 5 minutes.

Remove the roll from the refrigerator and unwrap the baking paper – this will create the pieces of chocolate 'bark'. Place the chocolate bark garnish on top of the cheesecake and dust with cocoa powder to finish. This cheesecake will keep in the refrigerator for up to 3 days.

CHOCOLATE ROLL

SERVES: 10-12 **DIFFICULTY:** 🍫🍫🍫

If you're looking for a kitchen challenge, this chocolate roll is ideal. Although the individual elements are not difficult to make, the whole process can be time consuming.

DÉCOR PASTE

50 g (1¾ oz) unsalted butter
50 g (1¾ oz) icing (confectioners') sugar
1–2 drops yellow food colouring
50 g (1¾ oz/about 2) egg whites
50 g (1¾ oz/⅓ cup) plain (all-purpose) flour

Using an electric mixer with a paddle attachment, beat the butter and icing sugar on low speed until the butter is softened and you have a smooth paste. Add the yellow food colouring followed by the egg whites and plain flour. Mix to combine.

Using a palette knife, spread the finished décor paste onto a non-stick baking mat approximately 40 x 30 cm (16 x 12 inches). Using a pastry comb, scrape it along the length of the mat to create individual lines. Alternatively, rather than using a comb, press your fingers firmly on the décor paste to create a pattern. Once you have created a design with the décor paste, place the mat on a flat tray and set the décor paste in the freezer for approximately 30 minutes.

CHOCOLATE SPONGE

180 g (6½ oz/about 3) whole eggs
90 g (3¼ oz) caster (superfine) sugar, plus extra for sprinkling
55 g (2 oz) plain (all-purpose) flour
30 g (1 oz/¼ cup) Dutch-process cocoa powder

Preheat the oven to 190°C (375°F). Put the eggs and sugar in a bowl over a saucepan of simmering water (ensuring the bowl doesn't touch the water) and heat the mixture to body temperature while whisking. Once the mixture reaches temperature, transfer to the bowl of an electric mixer with a whisk attachment and beat on high speed until light and creamy.

Sift the plain flour and cocoa powder together. Slowly add the sifted dry ingredients to the whipped eggs and sugar and gently fold them through with a spatula.

Remove the décor paste from the freezer and spread the chocolate sponge mixture evenly on top of the paste. Bake at for 7–8 minutes. If your fingers leave an impression in the sponge when touched, it's not ready. As soon as you remove the sponge from the oven, sprinkle it with caster sugar.

Place a piece of baking paper or a moist cloth over the sponge and flip the sponge over. Sprinkle the patterned side with caster sugar and flip it back so the patterned side is face down. With the baking paper or moist cloth still in place on top of the sponge roll the sponge into a tight roll. Set aside to cool. 👉

1. *Comb the décor paste onto a baking mat to create lines.*

2. *Spread the chocolate sponge on top of the chilled paste.*

3. *Spread the chocolate crème onto the sponge.*

CHOCOLATE CRÈME

115 g (4 oz) good-quality milk chocolate, coarsely chopped

115 g (4 oz) good-quality dark chocolate, coarsely chopped

80 g (2¾ oz/about 4) egg yolks

35 g (1¼ oz) caster (superfine) sugar

350 ml (12 fl oz) cream (35% fat)

150 g (5½ oz) unsalted butter

Put the two chocolates in a heatproof bowl. Whisk the egg yolks and sugar together in a heatproof bowl by hand. Put the cream in a saucepan over medium heat and bring it to the boil. Pour the hot cream over the egg yolk and sugar mixture, whisking constantly. Return the mixture to the pan over low heat, stirring constantly until the temperature reaches 80°C (176°F). (If you don't have a sugar thermometer, dip a wooden spoon in the mixture, lift it out and draw a line through the mixture on the spoon with your finger. If the anglaise runs straight over the line, it's not ready. If the line holds without any drips, it's ready. Do this process quickly before the anglaise runs off the spoon.) Strain the anglaise immediately over the chocolate, whisking until the chocolate is completely melted. Place a piece of plastic wrap directly on the surface of the chocolate crème and allow to cool completely at room temperature.

Using an electric mixer with a whisk attachment, whip the butter on medium–high speed until light and aerated. Slowly add the cooled chocolate crème, scraping the side of the bowl as you go to ensure all the butter is incorporated.

YELLOW CHOCOLATE GARNISH

100 g (3½ oz) good-quality white chocolate, finely chopped
yellow oil-based powdered food colouring

Temper the chocolate (see pages 12–14). Sift in the yellow food colouring and stir vigorously to combine. Spread the yellow chocolate in an even, thin layer on a sheet of acetate and cover immediately with another sheet of acetate, pressing it into the surface of the chocolate. Before the chocolate sets, using various-sized round cutters, ranging from 5 to 20 mm (¼ to ¾ inch), press firmly on top of the plastic to create individual discs, still sealed within the two sheets of plastic. Place the chocolate garnishes between two flat trays and into the refrigerator for 15 minutes.

ASSEMBLY

Unroll the prepared sponge and spread three-quarters of the chocolate crème evenly over the surface using a spatula. Using baking paper or a cloth, roll up the sponge with the crème, making it as tight as possible. Place the chocolate roll, seam side down, on a tray and place it in the refrigerator to set for 20–30 minutes.

Once set, remove it from the refrigerator and, using a serrated-edged knife, cut a narrow V along the length of the centre of the roll. Put the remaining chocolate crème in a piping (icing) bag with a 1 cm (½ inch) plain nozzle and pipe individual drops along the V.

Finally, remove the plastic sheets from the yellow chocolate garnish and place the discs onto the piped decoration. This roulade is best eaten the same day it is made, either cold or at room temperature. To cut the roulade, use a warm knife.

4. *Roll the sponge using baking paper as a guide and to help the rolling process.*

5. *Use various-sized round cutters to create the yellow chocolate garnishes.*

6. *Pipe the chocolate crème along the centre of the roll.*

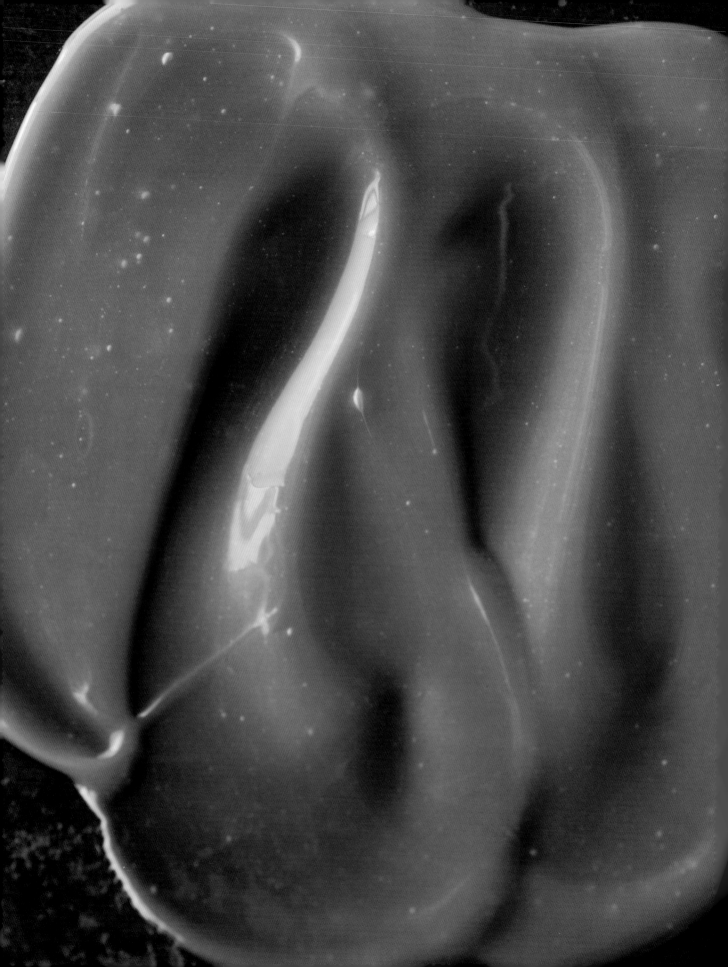

4.
TARTS

HOT CHOCOLATE TART

SERVES: 10-12 DIFFICULTY: 🍫

We start this chapter with the easiest tart and, in my opinion, one of the most delicious. You can make it up to three days in advance and store it covered in the refrigerator. It is best served hot and can be reheated in the microwave or oven before serving. It's quite rich so it will generously feed 10–12 people. I enjoy it best served with vanilla ice cream.

CHOCOLATE PASTRY

110 g (3¾ oz) unsalted butter

60 g (2¼ oz/½ cup) icing (confectioners') sugar

15 g (½ oz) Dutch-process cocoa powder

40 g (1½ oz/about 2) egg yolks

pinch of salt

20 g (¾ oz) almond meal

180 g (6½ oz) plain (all-purpose) flour, plus extra for dusting

½ teaspoon baking powder

Cream the butter, icing sugar and cocoa powder in the bowl of an electric mixer with a paddle attachment on medium speed. Add the egg yolks, mixing well and scraping down the side of the bowl as necessary. Add the dry ingredients. Mix only until the pastry comes together, then stop. Press the dough into an even, flat square, wrap it in plastic wrap and place it in the refrigerator to rest for 1 hour, or until firm.

Preheat the oven to 170°C (325°F). Roll out the dough on a lightly dusted work surface to a thickness of 3 mm (⅛ inch) and line the base and side of a 22 cm (8½ inch) tart ring (see pages 17–18). Place the tart shell in the refrigerator for 10 minutes to firm up. Using a small sharp knife, trim the top edge of the pastry so it's flush with the tin. Cut out a 25 cm (10 inch) circle of baking paper and crumple it into a ball. Open out the paper and use it to line the unbaked shell, then fill the shell with uncooked rice (see page 18). Bake for 7 minutes. Remove the tart from the oven and leave to cool at room temperature for 5 minutes. Remove the rice and paper.

CHOCOLATE FILLING

100 g (3½ oz/⅔ cup) coarsely chopped good-quality dark chocolate (80% cocoa solids)

10 g (⅜ oz) Dutch-process cocoa powder

120 g (4¼ oz) unsalted butter

180 g (6½ oz/about 3) whole eggs

130 g (4½ oz) caster (superfine) sugar

50 g (1¾ oz/⅓ cup) plain (all-purpose) flour, sifted

Melt the chocolate, cocoa powder and butter together in a double boiler or in a plastic bowl in the microwave (see page 12).

Preheat the oven to 180°C (350°F). In a bowl, lightly whisk the eggs and sugar by hand. Fold in the dark chocolate mixture, followed by the sifted flour. Continue gently folding using a spatula until well combined. Place the finished mixture into the par-baked tart shell and bake for 7–8 minutes. Let the tart cool at room temperature for 5 minutes before removing the tart ring. The tart is then ready to be sliced and served or stored in an airtight container in the refrigerator for up to 3 days.

CHOCOLATE MALLOW TART

SERVES: 10-12 **DIFFICULTY:**

Be warned – this is a rich tart best suited for an adult palate! If you find it too rich you can increase the number of marshmallows. Alternatively, if you're not a coffee lover, you can simply leave the coffee out. Finally, rather than bake one large tart, you can divide the mixture up between individual tart tins.

CHOCOLATE PASTRY

50 g (1¾ oz) unsalted butter

35 g (1¼ oz) icing (confectioners') sugar

20 g (¾ oz/about 1) egg yolk

10 g (⅜ oz) Dutch-process cocoa powder

pinch of salt

90 g (3¼ oz) plain (all-purpose) flour, plus extra for dusting

¼ teaspoon baking powder

Put the butter and icing sugar in the bowl of an electric mixer with a paddle attachment and mix on medium speed until the butter is completely smooth. Add the egg yolk, mixing well and scraping down the side of the bowl as necessary. Continue mixing on low speed and add 10 ml (¼ fl oz/2 teaspoons) water. Add the dry ingredients and mix until just combined. Press the dough into an even, flat square, wrap it in plastic wrap and place it in the refrigerator to rest for 1 hour, or until firm.

Preheat the oven to 170°C (325°F). Roll out the dough on a lightly dusted work surface to a thickness of 3 mm (⅛ inch) and line the base and side of a 22 cm (8½ inch) tart ring (see pages 17–18). Place the tart shell in the refrigerator for 10 minutes to firm up. Using a small sharp knife, trim the top edge of the pastry so it's flush with the tin. Cut out a 25 cm (10 inch) circle of baking paper and crumple it into a ball. Open out the paper and use it to line the unbaked shell, then fill the shell with uncooked rice (see page 18). Bake for 8 minutes. Remove the paper and rice and bake for a further 8 minutes. Remove the tart from the oven and leave to cool completely at room temperature.

CHOCOLATE MARSHMALLOW FILLING

225 ml (7½ fl oz) cream (35% fat)

pinch of salt

15 g (½ oz) roasted coffee beans, crushed

190 g (6¾ oz) good-quality dark chocolate, finely chopped

15 ml (½ fl oz/3 teaspoons) butterscotch schnapps

35 g (1¼ oz) marshmallows, chopped into quarters

Put the cream and salt in a saucepan over medium heat and bring to the boil. Remove the pan from the heat and add the crushed coffee beans. Cover the saucepan and leave to infuse at room temperature for 25 minutes.

Put the chocolate in a heatproof bowl. Strain the cream into a clean saucepan over medium heat and bring to the boil again. Pour the cream over the chocolate and whisk until the chocolate is melted and combined to create a ganache. Whisk in the butterscotch schnapps. Fold through the marshmallows. Spoon the ganache into the baked tart shell. Place the tart in the refrigerator for the ganache to set for at least 1½ hours prior to serving. You can store this tart in an airtight container in the refrigerator for up to 2 days.

PASSIONFRUIT MERINGUE TARTS

MAKES: 12 DIFFICULTY: ◆

A beautiful combination of textures and flavours makes these the perfect tarts for many occasions. Keep all the components separate and assemble as close to serving as you can to best appreciate the different textures.

130 g (4½ oz) unsalted butter
130 g (4½ oz) soft brown sugar
1 teaspoon salt
60 g (2¼ oz/about 3) egg yolks
185 g (6½ oz/1¼ cups) plain (all-purpose) flour, plus extra for dusting
15 g (½ oz) baking powder

BRETON SHORTBREAD

Using an electric mixer with a paddle attachment, beat the butter, sugar and salt on medium speed until combined. Add the egg yolks, mixing well and scraping down the side of the bowl as necessary, and finally the flour and baking powder, mixing until a dough forms. Press the dough into an even, flat square, wrap it in plastic wrap and place it in the refrigerator to rest for 1 hour, or until firm.

Preheat the oven to 170°C (325°F) and line a tray with a non-stick mat or baking paper. Remove the dough from the refrigerator. Lightly dust a work surface with flour and roll out the pastry to a 1 cm (½ inch) thickness. Using an 8 cm (3¼ inch) tart ring as your cutter, cut out 12 discs. Place the discs on the tray. Place an 8 cm (3¼ inch) tart ring around the outside of each pastry disc. Don't grease the tart rings. Bake for approximately 7–9 minutes until golden brown. Remove the tarts from the oven and, while still warm, run a knife around the inside of the tart rings to remove them. Cool the shortbread at room temperature. This shortbread can be frozen, well wrapped in plastic wrap prior to baking, and can be kept in the freezer for up to 4 weeks. Once baked, it is best to keep it in an airtight container at room temperature and eat it within a few days. ☞

1. *Cut the pastry into flat discs.*

2. *Place the rings onto the pastry discs for baking.*

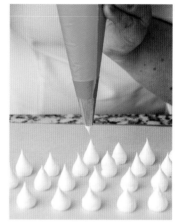

3. *Pipe the meringue puffs.*

PASSIONFRUIT CREAM

90 g (3¼ oz) good-quality white chocolate, coarsely chopped
120 ml (4 fl oz) passionfruit juice (from about 12 passionfruits)
265 g (9½ oz) caster (superfine) sugar
220 g (7¾ oz/about 11) egg yolks
1 teaspoon salt
165 g (5¾ oz) unsalted butter, chopped

Put the white chocolate in a heatproof bowl. To make passionfruit juice, cut open the passionfruits, scoop out the pulp and sieve out the seeds. Measure out 120 ml (4 fl oz) passionfruit juice. Put the juice, sugar, egg yolks and salt in a saucepan over low heat and whisk vigorously until the mixture boils. Boil for 1 minute, whisking constantly. Remove the pan from the heat and strain the mixture over the white chocolate. Whisk by hand to combine.

Transfer to the bowl of an electric mixer with a whisk attachment and mix in the butter, one piece at a time on low speed (this can also be done by hand with a spoon). Once all the butter is incorporated, press a piece of plastic wrap onto the surface of the cream and place in the refrigerator until required. The passionfruit cream can be made in advance and stored in the refrigerator for up to 3 days. It can also be stored in jars and used as a spread or dessert topping.

75 g (2¾ oz/about 3) egg whites

pinch of cream of tartar

110 g (3¾ oz/½ cup) caster (superfine)
sugar

60 g (2¼ oz/½ cup) icing (confectioners')
sugar, sifted, plus extra for dusting

15 g (½ oz) cornflour (cornstarch), sifted

30 g (1 oz/⅓ cup) desiccated (shredded)
coconut

SWISS MERINGUE PUFFS

Put the egg whites, cream of tartar and caster sugar in a mixing bowl. (If you are using an electric mixer, use the bowl from the mixer.) Choose a saucepan for the next step, ensuring the bowl can sit snugly over the water without coming into contact with it. Half-fill the saucepan with water and bring it to the boil, then turn off the heat. Sit the bowl on top of the saucepan, whisking lightly by hand until the mixture becomes warm to the touch. Remove the pan from the heat and use an electric mixer with a whisk attachment on high speed to create a meringue. Fold through the sifted icing sugar and cornflour gently using a spatula.

Preheat the oven to 60°C (140°F) and line a baking tray with a non-stick mat or baking paper.

Transfer the mixture to a piping (icing) bag with an 8 mm (⅜ inch) plain nozzle and pipe 5–10 mm (¼ –½ inch) meringues onto the lined baking tray, 1.5 cm (⅝ inch) apart. Sprinkle with the desiccated coconut and bake for approximately 1 hour 15 minutes or until dry and crunchy.

The Swiss meringue puffs can be made up to a week prior to use and stored in an airtight container. If they become sticky, just dry them out in a 90°C (195°F) oven for 20 minutes.

ASSEMBLY

Ensure the tart bases are cool. Using an ice-cream scoop or a spoon dipped in hot water, scoop the passionfruit cream into the centre of the tarts. Place meringue puffs on the surface of the passionfruit cream just prior to serving.

COCONUT, RASPBERRY & CHOCOLATE TARTS

MAKES: 8   DIFFICULTY: 🍫

If you want to simplify this recipe you can replace the made raspberry jelly with a good-quality store bought raspberry or berry jam.

COCONUT SHORTBREAD PASTRY

90 g (3¼ oz) unsalted butter
60 g (2¼ oz/½ cup) icing (confectioners') sugar
15 g (½ oz) almond meal
20 g (¾ oz) desiccated (shredded) coconut
30 g (1 oz/about ½) whole egg
160 g (5½ oz) plain (all-purpose) flour, plus extra for dusting
¼ teaspoon baking powder
¼ teaspoon salt

Using an electric mixer with a paddle attachment, beat the butter on medium speed until it is a thick, smooth paste. Sift in the icing sugar then add the almond meal, desiccated coconut and the egg and mix to combine. Add the flour, baking powder and salt and mix to combine until it comes together. Wrap in plastic wrap and place it in the refrigerator to rest for 1 hour, or until firm.

Preheat the oven to 160°C (315°F). Place eight individual 8 cm (3¼ inch) tart rings on a baking tray lined with baking paper.

Lightly dust a work surface with flour and roll out the dough to a thickness of 3 mm (⅛ inch) then line each tart ring with the rolled pastry (see pages 17–18). Place a large baking paper case in each tart ring and fill with uncooked rice (see page 18). Blind bake for approximately 6 minutes, then remove the paper case and rice and bake the tarts for a further 6 minutes or until light golden brown. You can freeze them, baking them as needed. Remove the tarts from the oven, allow to cool then remove the tart rings. The baked tarts can be made up to 3 days in advance and stored in an airtight container at room temperature.

CHOCOLATE MOUSSE

180 g (6½ oz) good-quality dark chocolate, coarsely chopped
50 ml (1¾ fl oz) cream (35% fat) (a)
70 ml (2¼ fl oz) coconut cream
½ teaspoon vanilla bean paste
160 ml (5¼ fl oz) cream (35% fat) (b)

Put the chocolate in a heatproof bowl. Put the cream (a), coconut cream and vanilla bean paste in a saucepan over medium heat and bring to the boil. Pour the hot mixture over the chocolate, whisking by hand until the chocolate is melted and completely combined with the cream, creating a ganache.

Place the cream (b) in a chilled bowl and whisk to a semi-whipped consistency (see page 16). Immediately and gently fold the semi-whipped cream through the ganache using a spatula until combined.

RASPBERRY JELLY

4 g (⅛ oz) gold-strength gelatine sheets
or 6 g (³⁄₁₆ oz) powdered gelatine
110 g (3¾ oz) frozen raspberries
80 g (2¾ oz) caster (superfine) sugar

Soak the gelatine sheets in a bowl of iced water and, once pliable, gently squeeze the sheets to remove any excess water. Set the sheets aside and leave at room temperature. If using the powder, sprinkle it over a bowl containing 30 ml (1 fl oz/1½ tablespoons) cold water. Leave at room temperature until needed.

Combine the frozen raspberries with the sugar in a saucepan over medium heat. Cook until the sugar is dissolved and the mixture comes to a gentle boil. Remove from the heat and add the gelatine, stirring until it is dissolved and combined.

FINISHING

Dutch-process cocoa powder, for dusting
shaved coconut, for garnishing
fresh raspberries, for garnishing

Evenly divide the raspberry jelly among the cooled tarts. Spoon the prepared chocolate mousse on top of the raspberry jelly to fill the tarts. Create a rough texture on the surface of the tart. Dust each tart with cocoa powder and garnish with shaved coconut and fresh raspberries. Eat immediately or store in an airtight container in the refrigerator for up to 24 hours.

Coconut, Raspberry & Chocolate Tarts PAGE 122

Baked Chocolate Peach Tart PAGE 126

BAKED CHOCOLATE PEACH TART

SERVES: 8–10 DIFFICULTY:

I like to use fresh, seasonal fruits for this recipe — stone fruits, blueberries and even apples are especially well suited. This beautiful tart can be served either cold in summer or hot in winter, when it can be reheated in the oven.

95 g (3¼ oz) unsalted butter

45 g (1½ oz) icing (confectioners') sugar, sifted

30 g (1 oz/about ½) whole egg

40 g (1½ oz) hazelnut meal

½ teaspoon salt

95 g (3¼ oz) plain (all-purpose) flour, plus extra for dusting

HAZELNUT SHORTBREAD

Using an electric mixer with a paddle attachment, beat the butter and icing sugar on medium speed until smooth. Add the egg followed by the dry ingredients. Mix until it comes together as a dough. Press the dough into an even, flat square, wrap it in plastic wrap and place it in the refrigerator to rest for 1 hour, or until firm.

Roll out the dough on a lightly floured work surface to a thickness of 3 mm (⅛ inch) and line the base and side of a 22 cm (8½ inch) tart ring (see pages 17–18). Place the tart shell in the refrigerator for 1 hour to firm up.

Preheat the oven to 170°C (325°F). Using a small sharp knife, trim the top edge of the pastry so it's flush with the tin. Cut out a 25 cm (10 inch) circle of baking paper and crumple it into a ball. Open out the paper and use it to line the unbaked shell, then fill the shell with uncooked rice (see page 18). Bake for 8–10 minutes. Remove the tart from the oven and leave to cool at room temperature for 5 minutes. Remove the paper and rice.

20 g (¾ oz) caster (superfine) sugar (a)

35 g (1¼ oz/¼ cup) custard powder

65 g (2¼ oz/¼ cup) mascarpone

35 g (1¼ oz) unsalted butter, softened, diced

105 g (3¾ oz) good-quality white chocolate, coarsely chopped

155 ml (5¼ fl oz) milk

90 ml (3 fl oz) cream (35% fat)

zest of 1 orange

½ teaspoon vanilla bean paste

90 g (3¼ oz/about 4) egg whites

¼ teaspoon cream of tartar

55 g (2 oz/¼ cup) caster (superfine) sugar (b)

2 red peaches or alternative fruit (I used Indian blood peaches for this tart. They are available from specialist greengrocers and turn an incredible shade of purple when baked.)

CREAM FILLING

Combine the caster sugar (a) and custard powder in a bowl and whisk together until combined (this process will help to eliminate lumps). Add the mascarpone and butter and stir them through. Put the chocolate in a heatproof bowl.

Put the milk, cream, orange zest and vanilla bean paste in a saucepan over medium heat and bring to the boil. Pour the hot mixture over the mascarpone mixture then return it all to the pan and, while stirring, heat until it reaches 80°C (176°F). Strain immediately over the white chocolate and whisk together until combined.

Using an electric mixer with a whisk attachment, whisk the egg whites with the cream of tartar on high speed until medium to firm peaks form. Gradually add the caster sugar (b), whisking until the sugar is dissolved. Fold the whipped egg whites through the prepared custard mixture by hand, using a spatula.

Preheat the oven to 180°C (350°F). Pour the finished cream filling into the par-baked tart case. Remove the stones from the red peaches, cut them into wedges and place them on the surface of the tart. Bake for 18–20 minutes until the cream filling becomes a light golden brown colour. The cream filling will rise up in the oven and collapse again once cool. The tart can be stored in an airtight container in the refrigerator for up to 2 days.

CHOCOLATE PECAN TART

SERVES: 8-10 DIFFICULTY: 🍫🍫

Depending on your preference, this tart is beautiful served either hot or cold. You can serve it as is or lightly dust the edge with sugar and cocoa powder, and a drizzle of cream.

SHORTBREAD

110 g (3¾ oz/¾ cup) plain (all-purpose) flour, plus extra for dusting
60 g (2¼ oz) unsalted butter, diced
40 g (1½ oz) caster (superfine) sugar
30 g (1 oz/about ½) whole egg

Sift the flour into a bowl and add the butter then form a crumb either using an electric mixer with a paddle attachment or by rubbing the butter into the flour by hand. It is important that you do not over-mix at this stage. Ensure that all the butter is combined without bringing the mixture together to form a paste.

In a separate bowl, combine the sugar, 1 teaspoon water and the egg and whisk to combine. Add this mixture to the crumb mixture and stir in until a smooth dough is formed, without excessive mixing. Press the dough into an even, flat square, wrap it in plastic wrap and place it in the refrigerator to rest for 1 hour, or until firm.

Roll out the dough on a lightly floured work surface to a thickness of 3 mm (⅛ inch) and line the base and side of a 25 cm (10 inch) tart ring (see pages 17–18). Place the tart shell in the refrigerator for 15 minutes to firm up.

Preheat the oven to 170°C (325°F). Using a small sharp knife, trim the top edge of the pastry so it's flush with the tin. Cut out a 30 cm (12 inch) circle of baking paper and crumple it into a ball. Open out the paper and use it to line the unbaked shell, then fill the shell with uncooked rice (see page 18). Bake for 8–10 minutes, until it is partially baked. Remove the paper case and rice, return to the oven and continue to bake for a further 5 minutes. Remove the tart shell from the oven and leave to cool at room temperature. 👉

1. *Melt the sugar until it is fully caramelised.*

2. *Once the sugar has caramelised, pour in the boiled cream.*

3. *Stir the mixture to combine.*

45 g (1½ oz) good-quality dark
  chocolate, coarsely chopped
100 ml (3½ fl oz) milk
100 ml (3½ fl oz) cream (35% fat)
40 g (1½ oz/about 2) egg yolks
20 g (¾ oz) soft brown sugar
15 g (½ oz/2 teaspoons) honey
15 g (½ oz) unsalted butter, melted
¼ teaspoon vanilla bean paste

BAKED CHOCOLATE CUSTARD

Preheat the oven to 90°C (195°F). Put the chocolate in a heatproof bowl. Put the milk and cream in a saucepan over medium heat and bring to the boil. Pour the hot cream over the chocolate, whisking until the chocolate is completely melted.

In a separate bowl, whisk together the egg yolks, sugar, honey, melted butter and vanilla bean paste. Add the chocolate mixture and whisk lightly by hand until combined. Pour the chocolate custard mixture into the par-baked tart case on a baking tray. Bake for 60–65 minutes, until the mixture just stops wobbling when you shake the baking tray. Leave at room temperature to cool.

90 g (3¼ oz) pecans

ROASTED PECANS

Preheat the oven to 160°C (315°F) and line a baking tray with baking paper. Roughly chop the pecans, place them on the lined tray and bake for 8–10 minutes. Set aside to cool.

CARAMEL

45 g (1½ oz) honey
150 ml (5 fl oz) cream (35% fat)
zest of 2 lemons
½ vanilla bean, seeds scraped
45 g (1½ oz) liquid glucose
5 g (³⁄₁₆ oz) salt
120 g (4¼ oz) caster (superfine) sugar
60 g (2¼ oz) good-quality white
   chocolate, coarsely chopped

Put the honey, cream, lemon zest, vanilla bean seeds, glucose and salt in a saucepan over medium heat and bring to the boil. Turn off the heat and keep warm.

Put the caster sugar in a wide-based saucepan over medium heat. Gently stir until the sugar is dissolved and fully caramelised to a light golden brown. (If the caramel starts to darken too quickly before all the sugar is dissolved, lower the heat.) Remove the pan from the heat and whisk in the warm cream mixture, which will stop the caramel cooking.

Put the chocolate in a bowl and strain the caramel over the chocolate, whisking by hand until combined.

ASSEMBLY

Arrange the roasted pecans onto the baked chocolate custard. Pour the prepared caramel over the pecans to evenly cover. Once you place the caramel on top of the tart, it is best eaten within 2 days and stored in the refrigerator. I prefer it served as soon as the hot caramel goes on.

4. *Strain the hot caramel over the white chocolate.*

5. *Pour the prepared caramel into the tart shell.*

BAKED CUSTARD APPLE TART

SERVES: 10 **DIFFICULTY:** ◼◼

Custard, apple and flaky pastry – what a brilliant combination! Serve the tart hot, either straight from the oven or reheated, with a drizzle of fresh cream or vanilla ice cream.

PIE PASTRY

160 g (5½ oz) plain (all-purpose) flour, plus extra for dusting
25 g (1 oz) cornflour (cornstarch)
95 g (3¼ oz) unsalted butter
10 g (⅜ oz) caster (superfine) sugar
pinch of salt
130 ml (4½ fl oz) cream (35% fat)

Preheat the oven to 200°C (400°F). Mix the flour, cornflour and butter in the bowl of an electric mixer with a paddle attachment on low speed, until you have a crumb, or do this by hand with your fingers. Add the sugar, salt and cream. Continue mixing until the dough comes together. Press the dough into an even, flat square, wrap it in plastic wrap and place it in the refrigerator to rest for 1 hour, or until firm.

Roll out two-thirds of the dough on a lightly floured work surface to a thickness of 4 mm (³⁄₁₆ inch) and line the base and side of a 20 cm (8 inch) tart ring (see pages 17–18). Brush the excess flour off the scraps, fold them gently and put them with the remaining one-third of pastry. Wrap in plastic wrap and place the tart shell and the remaining dough in the refrigerator for 20 minutes to firm up.

WHITE CHOCOLATE AND CINNAMON CUSTARD

45 g (1½ oz) good-quality white chocolate, coarsely chopped
20 g (¾ oz) cornflour (cornstarch)
90 g (3¼ oz) caster (superfine) sugar
40 g (1½ oz/about 2) egg yolks
75 ml (2½ fl oz) cream (35% fat) (a)
35 ml (1¼ fl oz) milk
¼ teaspoon vanilla bean paste
1 cinnamon stick
70 g (2½ oz) butter, diced
35 ml (1¼ fl oz) cream (35% fat) (b)

Put the chocolate in a heatproof bowl. In a separate bowl, whisk together the cornflour and sugar before adding the egg yolks and mixing well. Put the cream (a), milk, vanilla bean paste and cinnamon stick in a saucepan over medium heat and bring to the boil. Pour the cream mixture over the egg mixture, remove the cinnamon stick, and whisk to combine. Return the mixture to the pan and whisk until it comes to the boil. Continue to boil for 2–3 minutes to ensure the cornflour is cooked. Strain the mixture over the chocolate and whisk by hand to combine. Continue whisking and add the butter, one piece at a time – you can also use an electric mixer for this step. Cover with plastic wrap touching the surface of the custard and leave to cool at room temperature. Once cool, fold through cream (b) by hand using a spatula.

1. *Spread the cooled custard into the tart case.*

2. *Place the cooked apple slices on top.*

3. *Cover the apples with latticed pastry.*

APPLE PREPARATION

4 granny smith apples
squeeze of lemon juice
5 g (³/₁₆ oz) butter
¼ teaspoon ground cinnamon

Peel, core and quarter the apples then slice them into wedges about 8 mm (³/₈ inch) in thickness. Place the apple immediately in a bowl of water with a squeeze of lemon juice to stop them browning.

Melt the butter in a large frying pan over medium heat. Drain the apple slices and add them to the pan with the ground cinnamon and sauté for 8–10 minutes or until tender.

ASSEMBLY

1 egg yolk
30 ml (1 fl oz) milk
pinch of salt

Cover the base of the pastry shell with a layer of custard about 1 cm (½ inch) in thickness. Cover the custard with a layer of sliced apples followed by another layer of custard. Finish with the remaining sliced apples. Brush a small amount of water around the top edge of the tart to secure the top pastry.

Preheat the oven to 200°C (400°F). Roll out the remaining pastry to a 4 mm (³/₁₆ inch) thickness, then cut it into even 1 cm (½ inch) strips with a pizza cutter or sharp knife, ensuring that the strips are longer than the diameter of the tart. You need approximately 20 individual strips. Start by placing two strips of pastry over the tart to create a cross. Continue placing the strips over and under one another to create a lattice pattern. Press the base pastry and the lattice strips together by pinching them on the edge. Pinch the edges with your thumb and pointer finger. Trim away any overhanging pastry with a small, sharp knife. Mix together the egg yolk, milk and salt and brush the mixture over the top with a pastry brush.

Bake for approximately 40 minutes. This tart is best eaten the same day. Keep any leftovers in an airtight container in the refrigerator and heat again briefly in the oven before serving.

Baked Custard Apple Tart PAGE 134

ORANGE CHOCOLATE CARAMEL TART

SERVES: 8 DIFFICULTY: 🍫🍫

It's best to assemble this rustic-looking tart just before serving, which is relatively straightforward as all the individual components can be prepared in advance.

ORANGE CHOCOLATE SHORTBREAD

85 g (3 oz) unsalted butter

85 g (3 oz) caster (superfine) sugar

zest of 1 orange

½ teaspoon salt

40 g (1½ oz/about 2) egg yolks

95 g (3¼ oz) plain (all-purpose) flour, plus extra for dusting

20 g (¾ oz) Dutch-process cocoa powder

5 g (³⁄₁₆ oz) baking powder

Put the butter, sugar, orange zest and salt in the bowl of an electric mixer with a paddle attachment, and mix on medium speed until combined. Add the egg yolks, mixing well and scraping down the side of the bowl as necessary. Finally add the flour, cocoa powder and baking powder and mix until you have formed a dough. Press the dough into an even, flat square, wrap it in plastic wrap and place it in the refrigerator to rest for 1 hour, or until firm.

Preheat the oven to 160°C (315°F) and line a baking tray with baking paper. Roll out the dough on a lightly floured work surface to a thickness of 5 mm (¼ inch). Cut out a 20 cm (8 inch) diameter disc and place it on the baking tray. Place a 20 cm (8 inch) tart ring around the outside of the pastry disc. (The tart ring does not need greasing.) Bake for 10–12 minutes, until it rises. While the tart is still warm, run a knife around the inside edge of the tart ring to remove it. Cool the shortbread base at room temperature. This shortbread can be frozen prior to baking for up to 4 weeks. Once baked, it is best to keep it in an airtight container and eat it within a few days.

CARAMEL ORANGE CREAM

60 ml (2 fl oz/¼ cup) cream (35% fat)

zest of 1 orange

70 g (2½ oz) caster (superfine) sugar

20 g (¾ oz) liquid glucose

75 g (2¾ oz) unsalted butter

Put the cream and orange zest in a saucepan over medium heat and bring to the boil. Remove the pan from the heat, cover and keep warm.

Put the sugar in a large heavy-based saucepan over medium heat and stir gently until the sugar is fully dissolved and caramelised and you have achieved a light caramel colour. Remove the pan from the heat and, whisking constantly, add the hot orange cream immediately to stop the caramel cooking. (Be careful when adding the cream as it will generate a lot of steam and increase in volume very quickly.) Add the glucose and butter and whisk until combined. Put the mixture in a bowl and cover the caramel with plastic wrap so it is touching the surface. You can use the caramel immediately or you can leave it at room temperature for up to 4 days. ☞

45 g (1½ oz) good-quality milk
  chocolate, coarsely chopped
60 g (2¼ oz) good-quality dark
  chocolate, coarsely chopped
30 g (1 oz/about 1½) egg yolks
15 g (½ oz) caster (superfine) sugar
140 ml (4¾ fl oz) cream (35% fat)

Put the two chocolates together in a heatproof bowl. In a separate bowl, mix the egg yolks and sugar together by hand with a whisk. Put the cream in a saucepan over medium heat and bring to the boil. Pour the hot cream over the egg and sugar mixture and whisk to combine. Return the mixture to the pan and cook over low heat, stirring continuously with a spatula, until the mixture reaches 80°C (176°F) and produces an anglaise. (If you don't have a sugar thermometer, dip a wooden spoon in the mixture, lift it out and draw a line through the mixture on the spoon with your finger. If the anglaise runs straight over the line, it's not ready. If the line holds without any drips, it's ready. Do this process quickly before the anglaise runs off the spoon.) Immediately strain the anglaise over the chocolate and whisk until the chocolate is melted. Transfer to a bowl, or preferably a rectangular container, and cover with plastic wrap directly touching the surface of the creamer. Place in the refrigerator to set for 1–1½ hours.

1. Melt the sugar until it is fully caramelised.

2. Once the sugar has caramelised, pour in the boiled cream.

3. Stir the mixture to combine.

4. *Test the anglaise by running a finger across the spoon – if the line holds, the anglaise is ready.*

5. *Remove the pith and segment an orange for garnishing.*

6. *Create curls of chocolate creamer with a warm spoon.*

POACHED ORANGE

1 navel orange
70 g (2½ oz) caster (superfine) sugar

Peel the orange and, using a sharp knife, cut off both ends. Cut out individual orange segments from half the orange by cutting in between the membrane on both sides, removing as much pith as possible, and set the orange segments aside on paper towel. Reserve the remaining orange half for another use.

Put the sugar and 50 ml (1¾ fl oz) water in a saucepan over medium heat and cook until the sugar is dissolved. Remove the pan from the heat. Submerge the orange segments in the hot syrup and then gently drain and transfer to paper towel to absorb any excess moisture. Set aside until just before serving.

ASSEMBLY

Assemble the tart immediately before serving. Spread the caramel orange cream over the surface of the shortbread base with a spoon, without going over the edge. Dip a dessertspoon in hot water before cupping it along the surface of the chocolate creamer, creating individual curls of cream. Dip the spoon in water each time before scooping. Arrange the orange segments in between the curls.

BUTTERSCOTCH CHOCOLATE MERINGUE TARTS

MAKES: 10   **DIFFICULTY:** ◼◼

Using an upturned muffin tray is a really fantastic technique for creating tart shells. Line your flat discs of pastry as evenly as you can onto the tray so you don't end up with wonky tart shells. Simply delicious served on their own, these tarts make a great dessert or afternoon tea treat.

100 g (3½ oz) unsalted butter

40 g (1½ oz) soft brown sugar

20 g (¾ oz/about 1) egg yolk

145 g (5 oz) plain (all-purpose) flour, plus extra for dusting

¼ teaspoon baking powder

pinch of salt

150 g (5½ oz) dark chocolate, for lining tart shells

BUTTERSCOTCH PASTRY

Using an electric mixer with a paddle attachment, beat the butter and sugar on medium speed until the butter is completely smooth. Add the egg yolk, mixing well and scraping down the side of the bowl as necessary, and 15 ml (½ fl oz/3 teaspoons) water, followed by the sifted dry ingredients, except the chocolate, and mix until a dough forms. Press the dough into an even, flat square, wrap it in plastic wrap and place it in the refrigerator to rest for 1 hour, or until firm.

Preheat the oven to 160°C (315°F) and line a tray with baking paper. Roll out the dough on a lightly floured work surface to a thickness of 4 mm (³⁄₁₆ inch). Using an 8 cm (3¼ inch) cutter, cut out eight discs. Place the flat pastry discs on the tray and then freeze for 15 minutes to firm up.

Once frozen, place each disc over a muffin shape on an upturned muffin tray. (If both sides of the muffin tray are not teflon-coated, lightly grease the back of the tray with a little butter.) Bake for 8–10 minutes until golden brown. Remove the tart shells from the oven and leave at room temperature for 15 minutes. Gently remove the tart shells from the muffin tray and turn them the right way up.

Once the tarts have cooled completely, melt the chocolate in a double boiler or in a plastic bowl in the microwave (see page 12). Using a pastry brush, gently coat the inside of the tart shells with an even layer of chocolate. (This will help to stop the tart absorbing moisture from the filling.) Before being baked, the pastry can be stored in the refrigerator for up to 3 days, or frozen for 2 weeks prior to rolling out. You can also refrigerate or freeze the rolled and cut discs before baking. ☛

CARAMELISED BANANAS

10 ml (¼ fl oz/2 teaspoons) lemon juice
70 g (2½ oz) caster (superfine) sugar
1 vanilla bean, seeds scraped
30 g (1 oz/1 tablespoon) liquid glucose
2 bananas, diced into 1 cm (½ inch)
   cubes
55 ml (1¾ fl oz) cream (35% fat)
40 g (1½ oz) unsalted butter

Put the lemon juice, sugar, vanilla bean seeds and glucose in a frying pan over medium heat and stir gently until the sugar is dissolved and lightly caramelised. Add the banana and sauté for 2–3 minutes before stirring in the cream, followed by the butter. Stir gently until all the ingredients are incorporated. Put the finished caramelised banana in a bowl and cover with plastic wrap touching the surface of the banana mixture. Set aside at room temperature until required.

CHOCOLATE CUSTARD

300 ml (10½ fl oz) milk
1 vanilla bean, seeds scraped
10 g (⅜ oz) custard powder
60 g (2¼ oz) caster (superfine) sugar
80 g (2¾ oz/about 4) egg yolks
pinch of salt
65 g (2¼ oz) good-quality dark
   chocolate, coarsely chopped
75 g (2¾ oz) unsalted butter, diced

Put the milk and vanilla bean seeds in a saucepan over medium heat and bring to the boil. Keep warm. Whisk together the custard powder and sugar in a heatproof bowl to combine (this helps to avoid lumps), then add the egg yolks and salt. Pour the boiled milk over the egg mixture and whisk together before returning the mixture to the saucepan over medium heat and whisking while it comes back to the boil. Continue whisking for 1 minute, while boiling, to ensure the custard powder is cooked.

Put the chocolate in a heatproof bowl. Strain the hot milk mixture through a sieve over the chocolate and whisk to combine. Still whisking, add the butter, one small piece at a time. Once all the chocolate and butter is incorporated, press plastic wrap onto the surface of the custard and place in the refrigerator to cool. The chocolate custard can be stored in the refrigerator for up to 2 days.

1. *Take the pastry discs straight from the freezer and centre them on the over-turned muffin-tray holes.*

2. *Remove the tart shells once cool.*

3. *Lightly brush the inside of the tart shells with chocolate.*

MERINGUE

100 g (3½ oz/about 4) egg whites
½ teaspoon cream of tartar
225 g (8 oz) caster (superfine) sugar

Put the egg whites, cream of tartar and sugar in a heatproof bowl over a saucepan of simmering water (ensuring the bowl doesn't touch the water) and heat the mixture to body temperature while whisking. Once the mixture reaches temperature, transfer to the bowl of an electric mixer with a whisk attachment and beat on high speed until medium peaks form. Use this meringue as soon as possible after whisking – it is best to have the other two fillings in your tart before you start the meringue. If the meringue is rigid and difficult to place on the tart, give it a quick whisk by hand to soften it up, before placing it on the tart. Once all the tarts are topped with the meringue, it's optional to brown them with a blowtorch. (This recipe will create a little more meringue than you require for the tarts, because it is difficult to whisk smaller quantities of egg whites successfully. I recommend folding some fruit through the remaining meringue and serving it with some ice cream.)

ASSEMBLY

Spoon the caramelised banana into the shells about halfway up. Fill the tarts to the top with the chocolate custard by spooning it in. Finish by topping the tarts with the prepared meringue. These tarts are best eaten the same day they are assembled. The banana and the chocolate custard can be made up to 2 days before and kept in the refrigerator until you're ready to assemble the tarts.

4. *Spoon the meringue on top of the chocolate custard.*

5. *Toast the meringue lightly with a blowtorch.*

145

CRUNCHY LEMON & WHITE CHOCOLATE TARTS

MAKES: 8 DIFFICULTY: ◼◼ **GLUTEN-FREE**

Not only are these tarts delicious – a beautiful combination of sweet and tart, with a multitude of different textures – but gluten-free as well. This one is for my mum, who is a coeliac.

HAZELNUT DACQUOISE

25 g (1 oz) roasted hazelnuts
50 g (1¾ oz/about 2) egg whites
40 g (1½ oz) caster (superfine) sugar
pinch of cream of tartar
15 g (½ oz) hazelnut meal
15 g (½ oz) almond meal
40 g (1½ oz/⅓ cup) icing (confectioners') sugar, plus extra for dusting
1 teaspoon cornflour (cornstarch)

Preheat the oven to 160°C (315°F). Put the hazelnuts on a baking tray and roast them for 12–15 minutes until golden brown. When cool enough to handle, use a cloth to remove the skins by rubbing the surface of the hazelnut. Once cool, roughly chop the hazelnuts and set aside.

Using an electric mixer with a whisk attachment, beat the egg whites with one-third of the caster sugar and the cream of tartar on high speed until medium peaks form. Gradually add the remaining caster sugar and continue mixing for 1 minute until the sugar is completely dissolved. Sieve the hazelnut meal, almond meal, icing sugar and cornflour into a bowl (if you have any small pieces of nuts that don't go through the sieve you can still incorporate them into the mix) and fold this mixture into the meringue base using a spatula.

Preheat the oven to 160°C (315°F). Grease eight 8 cm (3¼ inch) tart rings (egg rings make perfect tart rings) and place them on a baking tray lined with baking paper. Put the prepared dacquoise mixture into a piping (icing) bag with a 1 cm (½ inch) plain nozzle. Swirl a full circle to fill the base of the ring, then pipe another ring around the outside to create a tart shape (this can also be done gently with a spoon). Dust some icing sugar on top and scatter over the chopped, roasted hazelnuts. Bake for approximately 20 minutes until light golden brown and the dacquoise feels firm to the touch. Remove from the oven and, while the dacquoise is still warm, run a knife directly around the inside edge of the tart rings and remove them. The dacquoise can be stored at room temperature in an airtight container for up to 2 days or frozen for up to 1 month. ☞

LEMON AND WHITE CHOCOLATE CURD

65 g (2¼ oz) good-quality white
   chocolate, coarsely chopped

75 ml (2½ fl oz) lemon juice

zest of 1 lemon

165 g (5¾ oz/¾ cup) caster (superfine)
   sugar

100 g (3½ oz/about 5) egg yolks

½ teaspoon salt

210 g (7½ oz) unsalted butter, chopped
   and softened

Put the chocolate in a heatproof bowl. Put the lemon juice, zest, sugar, egg yolks and salt in a saucepan over low heat and whisk vigorously until the mixture comes to the boil. Continue to boil for 1 minute, then strain the mixture over the chocolate, whisking until the chocolate is melted and combined. Add the butter slowly, one piece at a time, and whisk it in to combine. (This can also be done using an electric mixer.) If the mixture is cooling too quickly and all the butter is not incorporating, you can place the bowl of curd over a saucepan of simmering water and whisk by hand while adding the butter. Put a piece of plastic wrap on the surface of the curd and place in the refrigerator until required. This can be stored in the refrigerator for up to 3 days. It can also be placed in sterilised jars, sealed and used as a spread or dessert topping.

1. *Pipe the dacquoise into the greased ring.*

2. *Run a knife around the ring to release the dacquoise.*

FRENCH MERINGUE

75 g (2¾ oz/about 3) egg whites
pinch of cream of tartar
100 g (3½ oz) caster (superfine) sugar
yellow oil-based powdered food
  colouring

Preheat the oven to 100°C (200°F) and line a baking tray with baking paper. Put the egg whites and cream of tartar in the bowl of an electric mixer and whisk until medium to firm peaks form. Gradually add the caster sugar and continue whisking for a minute.

Take one-quarter of the meringue and colour it with enough yellow food colouring to achieve a bright yellow. Gently fold the coloured meringue through the white meringue to create a marbled effect. (Avoid over-mixing as you will lose the marbling effect.) Transfer the mixture to a piping (icing) bag with a 1 cm (½ inch) plain nozzle and pipe 5–10 mm (¼–½ inch) meringues onto the lined baking tray, 1.5 cm (⅝ inch) apart. Bake for approximately 2 hours or until crunchy. (You will create more meringues than you need, as it is difficult to whisk smaller volumes of egg white. The meringues will stay crunchy if stored in an airtight container for up to 3 weeks.)

ASSEMBLY

Put the lemon and white chocolate curd in a piping bag with a 1.2 cm (⁷⁄₁₆ inch) plain nozzle and swirl it onto the baked dacquoise base until it is just slightly higher than the top of the tart shell. Cover the lemon curd with the meringues and your tarts are ready to serve. (It is best to assemble this tart just a few hours prior to serving to maintain the crunchy texture in the base and the meringues.)

3. *Gently fold the two colours of meringue together to create a marbled effect.*

4. *Pipe the marbled meringue onto a lined tray.*

5.

AFTERNOON TEA

CHOCOLATE FUDGE SQUARES

MAKES: 60 DIFFICULTY: ◆ **GLUTEN-FREE**

You can change the flavour of this fudge recipe by simply adding in roasted nuts, such as pecans, walnuts and hazelnuts. Alternatively, boil the cream and infuse it overnight with 30 g (1 oz) of roasted coffee beans and then re-measure the cream to the original amount before proceeding with the recipe.

345 ml (11½ fl oz) cream (35% fat)

2 vanilla beans, seeds scraped

250 g (9 oz) caster (superfine) sugar

90 g (3¼ oz) liquid glucose

225 g (8 oz) unsalted butter

35 g (1¼ oz) honey

1 teaspoon salt

½ teaspoon bicarbonate of soda (baking soda)

110 g (3¾ oz/¾ cup) finely chopped good-quality dark chocolate

Line a 27 x 17.5 cm (10¾ x 7 inch) baking tin by spraying it with vegetable oil and lining the base and sides with a piece of baking paper. Put the cream and vanilla bean seeds in a saucepan over medium heat and bring to the boil. Remove from the heat, cover and keep warm.

Put the sugar, glucose and 50 ml (1¾ fl oz) water in a large saucepan and heat to 145°C (293°F). (If you don't have a sugar thermometer, use a teaspoon to take a small amount of the sugar syrup and drop it into a bowl of chilled water. If it is the correct temperature it will separate when it hits the water into hard, but pliable, threads that will bend slightly before breaking.) When at the correct temperature, immediately whisk in the butter and honey. Mixing continuously, pour in the boiling liquid cream, in two or three stages, to prevent the temperature of the sugar from dropping below 110°C (230°F). Add the salt and bicarbonate of soda and whisk to combine. Reheat the mixture over medium heat, while stirring, until it reaches 119°C (246°F). (If you don't have a sugar thermometer, drop a small amount into a bowl of chilled water and it should be a firm but pliable texture.) Once it reaches temperature, whisk in the dark chocolate vigorously, until it is completely melted, to ensure that the sugar crystallises to create a fudge texture when set. Pour immediately into your prepared baking tin. Leave at room temperature to set for approximately 5 hours. Use a lightly oiled knife to cut the fudge into 3 cm (1¼ inch) squares. It can be stored in an airtight container at room temperature for up to 1 month.

ALMOND CHOCOLATE CAKES

MAKES: 12   DIFFICULTY: 🍫 **GLUTEN-FREE**

I can't resist tormenting my work colleague Paul by making these cakes and watching him try to resist taking a bite! These little cakes will stay moist at room temperature or in the refrigerator for up to a week.

ALMOND CHOCOLATE CAKES

310 g (11 oz) marzipan (50% almonds)

60 g (2¼ oz) Dutch-process cocoa powder, sifted

170 g (6 oz/about 3) whole eggs, lightly beaten

85 g (3 oz) unsalted butter, just melted and not too hot

icing (confectioners') sugar, for dusting

Preheat the oven to 165°C (320°F). Put the marzipan and sifted cocoa powder in the bowl of an electric mixer with a paddle attachment and mix on low speed until combined. Slowly add the eggs in stages to the marzipan mixture, mixing well after each addition and scraping down the side of the bowl. Slowly add the melted butter, scraping down the side of the bowl as you go. Evenly divide the mixture between 12 holes in a greased or non-stick cupcake tray. Bake for approximately 12–15 minutes until a cake bounces back when touched. Remove from the oven and leave in the tin to cool at room temperature. Remove the cakes from the tray and make a 1.5 cm (⅝ inch) hole in the centre of the top of each cake with the handle of a teaspoon. Dust with icing sugar.

BERRY JAM

200 g (7 oz) frozen or fresh raspberries

125 g (4½ oz) caster (superfine) sugar

Put the raspberries in a saucepan over medium heat and bring to the boil, while stirring. Add the caster sugar, still stirring, and bring the mixture back to the boil. Continue to boil until the mixture reaches 102°C (216°F). (If you don't have a sugar thermometer, you can test the jam by dropping a small amount on a chilled plate and checking the consistency — it should just hold its shape.) Spoon a small amount of jam into the hole on the top of each chocolate cake. Store at room temperature for up to 4 days or in the refrigerator for up to a week.

CHOUX PASTRY

MAKES: 1 BATCH **DIFFICULTY:**

You'll find this simple and versatile choux pastry is called for in a number of the recipes in this chapter: Paris Brest (page 158); Chocolate caramel éclair (page 166); Choux puffs with lime coconut filling (page 174); and Chocolate coffee éclair (page 178).

65 ml (2¼ fl oz) milk

pinch of salt

5 g (³⁄₁₆ oz) caster (superfine) sugar

45 g (1½ oz) unsalted butter

70 g (2½ oz) plain (all-purpose) flour, sifted

120 g (4¼ oz/about 2) whole eggs, lightly beaten

Put the milk, 65 ml (2¼ fl oz) water, the salt, sugar and butter in a saucepan over medium heat and bring to the boil. Immediately remove the pan from the heat and whisk in the sifted flour. Vigorously stir the choux pastry then return the pan to the heat. Continue stirring until there is a light, oily sheen on the surface and the dough comes away from the side of the pan.

Remove the pan from the heat and transfer the mixture to the bowl of an electric mixer with a paddle attachment. Mixing on medium speed, add a small amount of the egg at a time, mixing after each addition until fully incorporated before adding any more. Once the mixture very slowly slides off a spoon, it is ready – don't add any more egg. This mixture can be kept in the refrigerator for up to 1 hour, covered with a slightly damp cloth.

1. *Stir until the choux mixture has a slight sheen.*

2. *The choux mixture should just slide off the spoon when enough egg is added.*

3. *Choux pastry can be used in a variety of recipes.*

PARIS BREST

MAKES: 8   DIFFICULTY: ◆

Paris Brest were originally designed to celebrate the cycling race from Paris to Brest in 1910 in France. The shape represents a bike wheel. These delicious doughnut-shaped morsels are easier to pipe than éclairs and have a more rustic appeal.

CHOUX PASTRY

25 g (1 oz/¼ cup) flaked almonds

Prepare one batch of choux pastry dough, following the recipe on page 156.

Preheat the oven to 170°C (325°F) and grease a baking tray with a small amount of butter or vegetable oil spray. Dust the tray lightly with flour and, using your finger or a plastic scraper, mark eight 7 cm (2¾ inch) rings where you will pipe your Paris Brest. Leave a 5 cm (2 inch) gap between them.

Put the prepared choux pastry in a piping (icing) bag with a 1.5 cm (⅝ inch) star-shaped nozzle. Pipe the choux pastry into rings on your tray, following your guidelines. If you have any peaks in your piping, dip your finger in water and tap them down. Sprinkle the top of each Paris Brest with flaked almonds. (You can freeze the Paris Brest before baking for up to 1 month.)

Place all the Paris Brest in the oven at the same time if possible. While baking, do not open the oven door. Bake for 10 minutes then reduce the temperature to 150°C (300°F) and bake for a further 15 minutes. Reduce the oven temperature to 130°C (250°F) and bake for a further 20 minutes or until the Paris Brest are firm and a dark golden brown on the outside. Once they are baked, open the oven door to release the steam and leave them in the oven to continue to dry them out for a few minutes.

CHOCOLATE AND RASPBERRY CHANTILLY

115 g (4 oz) good-quality milk chocolate, coarsely chopped
340 ml (11½ fl oz) cream (35% fat)
250 g (9 oz/2 cups) fresh or frozen raspberries

Put the chocolate in a heatproof bowl. Put the cream in a small saucepan over medium heat and bring to the boil. Pour the hot cream over the chocolate, whisking by hand until all the chocolate is melted and combined with the cream. Cover the bowl and place the mixture in the refrigerator for at least 2 hours.

Using an electric mixer with a whisk attachment, whip the chilled cream and chocolate mixture with the raspberries on high speed until you achieve a consistency that holds. (Because of the additional fat in the chocolate, this cream will easily split, so be careful not to over-whisk.) Store the cream in the refrigerator until ready to pipe.

ASSEMBLY

250 g (9 oz/2 cups) fresh raspberries, for garnishing
icing (confectioners') sugar, for dusting

Using a serrated knife, cut the Paris Brest in half horizontally. Separate the two pieces but keep the top with the base so you don't mix them up. Place the prepared chocolate and raspberry chantilly in a piping (icing) bag with a 1–1.5 cm (½–⅝ inch) star-shaped nozzle. Pipe the cream into the base of the Paris Brest, using a circular motion, trying to stay within the pastry. Place the fresh raspberries on top of the cream and place the tops on. Lightly dust with icing sugar just prior to serving. As with all choux pastry, Paris Brest is best eaten the day it is assembled. You can freeze the choux pastry, unfilled, for up to 1 month if in a sealed container.

Chocolate Meringue Kisses PAGE 162

CHOCOLATE MERINGUE KISSES

MAKES: 26 **DIFFICULTY:** ◆ **GLUTEN-FREE**

You can substitute the cocoa powder in this recipe for oil-based powdered food colouring and make colourful marbled meringues. All colours are different in strength so just add enough until you have the desired colour.

CHOCOLATE MERINGUE

60 g (2¼ oz/about 2½) egg whites
pinch of cream of tartar
60 g (2¼ oz) caster (superfine) sugar
60 g (2¼ oz/½ cup) icing (confectioners')
  sugar, sifted
10 g (⅜ oz) Dutch-process cocoa
  powder

Preheat the oven to 100°C (200°F) and line a baking tray with a non-stick mat or baking paper. Put the egg whites and cream of tartar in the bowl of an electric mixer with a whisk attachment and beat on high speed until medium peaks form. Gradually add the caster sugar and continue whisking until the sugar is dissolved, then fold through the icing sugar using a spatula.

Put one-third of this meringue in another bowl. Sift over the cocoa powder and fold it through until well combined. Marble this cocoa meringue through the remaining white meringue, by gently folding large spoonfuls of the cocoa meringue into the white meringue base and swirling it through gently, without completely mixing it together.

Transfer the marbled mixture to a piping (icing) bag with a 1.5 cm (⅝ inch) plain nozzle. Pipe 2.5–3 cm (1–1¼ inch) meringues onto the prepared tray, 1 cm (½ inch) apart. (If you don't have a piping bag, use a teaspoon.) Bake for approximately 1½ hours or until the meringue is crunchy right through to the centre. Leave on the tray at room temperature to cool. Once cool, place the meringues in an airtight container until you are ready to use them, or they can simply be eaten right away. They can be stored for up to 3 weeks without filling. If they become soft, dry them out in a 90°C (195°F) oven for 20 minutes.

150 g (5½ oz/1 cup) coarsely chopped
   good-quality dark chocolate
120 ml (4 fl oz) cream (35% fat)
30 g (1 oz/1 tablespoon) honey
1 teaspoon sea salt
1 teaspoon unsalted butter

CHOCOLATE CREAM FILLING

Put the chocolate in a heatproof bowl. Put the cream, honey and salt in a small saucepan over medium heat and bring to the boil. Pour the hot cream over the chocolate, whisking by hand until combined and the chocolate is melted. Add the butter and continue to whisk until incorporated. Cover the ganache with plastic wrap touching the surface. Leave at room temperature to set for 2–3 hours.

Take the prepared chocolate cream filling and place it in a piping (icing) bag with a 1 cm (½ inch) plain nozzle. Match up the meringues into pairs of similar size. Pipe (or spoon) the mixture onto one meringue then gently sandwich it together with another meringue. It is best to assemble the meringues no more than 12 hours prior to serving. Store in an airtight container once made until required.

CHOCOLATE TRUFFLE SQUARES

MAKES: 36 DIFFICULTY: ◆ **GLUTEN-FREE**

With crispy almonds, pistachios and dark chocolate, these are truffles at their best. A rich treat, more suitable for adult tastes, that are best served alongside coffee or tea.

CRISPY ALMONDS

125 g (4½ oz/1 cup) slivered almonds
35 g (1¼ oz) caster (superfine) sugar
icing (confectioners') sugar, for dusting

Preheat the oven to 160°C (315°F) and line a baking tray with a non-stick mat or baking paper. Put the slivered almonds in a bowl. Put the caster sugar and 25 ml (¾ fl oz) water in a small saucepan over medium heat and bring to the boil. Cook until the sugar is dissolved. Pour the prepared sugar syrup over the almonds and mix together to coat.

Place the slivered almonds on the prepared baking tray and dust with icing sugar. Roast in the oven for 15–18 minutes, turning the almonds every 5 minutes to ensure they roast evenly. Remove them from the oven and leave to cool at room temperature.

TRUFFLE SQUARES

60 g (2¼ oz) pistachio nuts
75 ml (2½ fl oz) cream (35% fat)
395 g (14 oz) condensed milk
30 g (1 oz) unsalted butter
400 g (14 oz/2⅔ cups) coarsely chopped good-quality dark chocolate
135 g (4¾ oz) crispy almonds (see recipe above)
Dutch-process cocoa powder, for dusting

Line a 20 cm (8 inch) square cake tin with baking paper. Preheat the oven to 160°C (315°F) and put the pistachio nuts on a baking tray lined with baking paper. Roast the pistachios for 8–10 minutes, then remove from the oven and leave to cool at room temperature.

Meanwhile, put the cream in a medium saucepan over medium heat and bring to the boil. Immediately add the condensed milk and butter and stir gently with a spatula over low heat for 2–3 minutes. Remove the pan from the heat, add the chocolate and stir to combine and melt the chocolate. Pour the mixture into a bowl and add the pistachio nuts and crispy almonds. Mix until combined then pour the mixture into the prepared tin. Place in the refrigerator for 3–4 hours to set. Dust with cocoa powder and slice into 3 cm (1¼ inch) squares. Store at room temperature (if under 24°C/75°F) in an airtight container for up to a week. If your room is hotter, store in the refrigerator.

CHOCOLATE CARAMEL ÉCLAIR

MAKES: 9 DIFFICULTY: 🍫🍫

Éclairs are best eaten the day they are assembled but both the éclairs and the chocolate crème can be pre-made and stored.

CHOUX PASTRY

Prepare one batch of choux pastry dough, following the recipe on page 156.

Preheat the oven to 170°C (325°F) and grease a baking tray with a small amount of butter or vegetable oil spray. Dust the tray lightly with flour and, using your finger or a plastic scraper, mark where you will pipe your éclairs, 10 cm (4 inches) in length, leaving a 5 cm (2 inch) gap between them.

Put the prepared choux pastry in a piping (icing) bag with a 1.5 cm (⅝ inch) star-shaped nozzle. Pipe the choux pastry into straight lines onto the tray, following your guidelines. If it is easier, cut the choux pastry with scissors or a small sharp knife into 10 cm (4 inch) lengths. (You can freeze the éclairs before baking for up to 1 month.)

Place all the piped éclairs in the oven at the same time if possible. While baking, do not open the oven door. Bake for 10 minutes then reduce the temperature to 150°C (300°F) and bake for a further 15 minutes. Reduce the oven temperature to 130°C (250°F) and bake for a further 20 minutes or until the éclairs are firm and a dark golden brown on the outside. Once the éclairs are baked, open the door to release the steam and leave them in the oven to continue to dry out for a few minutes. ☞

CHOCOLATE CRÈME

135 g (4¾ oz) good-quality dark
   chocolate, coarsely chopped
10 g (⅜ oz) custard powder
50 g (1¾ oz) caster (superfine) sugar
95 g (3¼ oz/about 5) egg yolks
245 ml (8½ fl oz) milk
½ teaspoon vanilla bean paste
70 g (2½ oz) unsalted butter, diced

Put the chocolate in a heatproof bowl. Whisk together the custard powder and sugar in a bowl then whisk in the egg yolks. Put the milk and vanilla bean paste in a medium saucepan over medium heat and bring to the boil. Pour the hot mixture over the egg mixture and whisk together before returning the mixture to the saucepan and whisking until it comes back to the boil. Pour the mixture over the chocolate, whisking until combined and the chocolate is melted. Whisk the butter into the crème by hand, a piece at a time. (This process can also be done using an electric mixer with a paddle attachment.) Once all the butter is added, press a piece of plastic wrap onto the surface of the crème and place it in the refrigerator to cool for approximately 1 hour. This chocolate crème can be stored for up to 3 days in the refrigerator prior to use.

TOFFEE

65 g (2¼ oz/2½ cups) puffed rice cereal
edible gold dust
400 g (14 oz) caster (superfine) sugar
80 g (2¾ oz/¼ cup) liquid glucose

This toffee topping is optional – you can simply dust the éclairs with icing sugar. You need to make more of this topping than you need, so you can dip all the éclairs thoroughly.

Place the puffed rice cereal in a bowl and coat it in a small amount of edible gold dust just to give it a light sheen.

Put the sugar and 160 ml (5¼ fl oz) water in a saucepan over medium heat and bring to the boil. You can stir the mixture until it starts boiling, then you must stop stirring. When the syrup is boiling, add the glucose. Increase the heat to high and cook until the syrup reaches 165°C (329°F), without stirring. (If you don't have a sugar thermometer, the sugar syrup is ready when the bubbles on the surface get smaller and become a pale golden colour.) Remove the pan from the heat and place it on a folded cloth sitting on a work surface. When the bubbles on the surface of the toffee dissipate, you are ready to dip.

Hold each éclair on the side horizontally, keeping your fingers close to the base. Dip the top of each éclair and place it, toffee side down, into the gold puffed rice cereal. Leave the éclairs in the puffed rice cereal to set for 30 seconds and then place them, pastry side down, on a lined tray. You can reheat the toffee once it becomes hard over low heat until it is liquid again.

Using a serrated knife, cut each éclair lengthways, without going all the way through. Place the prepared chocolate crème in a piping (icing) bag with a 1 cm (½ inch) star-shaped nozzle. Pipe the crème into the éclair, using a circular motion. (You can also spoon the crème in using a teaspoon.) These éclairs should be eaten within a few hours of being filled. (If you are in a humid climate, the toffee may dissolve within a couple of hours.) The éclairs, once baked and without filling or toffee, can be stored in an airtight container in the freezer for up to 4 weeks.

1. *Dip the baked éclairs into the toffee and then directly into the puffed rice cereal.*

2. *Cut the éclair on the side – not the whole way through.*

3. *Pipe chocolate crème inside.*

CHOCOLATE-GLAZED DOUGHNUTS

MAKES: 15 DIFFICULTY: 🍫🍫

Doughnuts are always a great way to influence people and win friends! Yeast doughs are sometimes daunting but this recipe makes the process simple. Enjoy these delicious baked goods on the day they're made for the ultimate doughnut experience.

190 ml (6½ fl oz) milk

35 g (1¼ oz) unsalted butter

35 ml (1¼ fl oz) warm water
 (approximately 35°C/95°F)

7 g (¼ oz) fresh yeast

60 g (2¼ oz/about 1) whole egg, beaten

40 g (1½ oz) caster (superfine) sugar

¾ teaspoon salt

¼ teaspoon ground cinnamon

340 g (12 oz) plain (all-purpose) flour,
 plus extra for dusting

vegetable oil, for deep-frying
 (approximately 3 litres/
 105 fl oz/12 cups)

DOUGHNUTS

Put the milk in a medium saucepan over low heat and heat until just warm. Remove from the heat. Add the butter and mix until it has melted.

Put the warm water in a bowl and sprinkle the yeast on top then let it sit for 5 minutes. Place this mixture in the bowl of an electric mixer with a paddle attachment. Add the warm milk and butter mixture, egg, sugar, salt and cinnamon and half the flour and beat on medium speed until it comes together as a dough. Change the paddle attachment to a dough hook, if you have one. Mix for 1 minute then add the remaining flour. Continue mixing for approximately 10 minutes, or until the dough pulls away from the side of the bowl. Transfer to a lightly oiled bowl and leave to rise for 1 hour at room temperature with a damp cloth draped over the top. Once it has risen to approximately double its size, punch the air out of the dough.

Lightly dust a work surface with flour and place the dough on top. Roll it out to a 3 cm (1¼ inch) thickness and cut either with a 6 cm (2½ inch) doughnut cutter or a 6 cm round cutter for the outside, and a 2 cm (¾ inch) cutter for the inside. As you cut them, put the doughnuts on a piece of baking paper lightly dusted with flour. Cover with a damp cloth and rest for a further 30 minutes.

Heat the vegetable oil in a deep-fryer or saucepan to 180°C (350°F) or until a cube of bread turns golden brown in the oil in 15 seconds. Once the oil reaches the desired temperature, place 2–3 doughnuts at a time in the oil and cook for approximately 1 minute on each side or until golden brown. Transfer to a tray lined with paper towel to drain, and leave to cool at room temperature for 20 minutes.

CHOCOLATE TOPPING

50 g (1¾ oz/⅓ cup) finely chopped
  good-quality dark chocolate
50 g (1¾ oz) unsalted butter, diced
80 ml (2½ fl oz/⅓ cup) milk
15 g (½ oz/2 teaspoons) liquid glucose
1 vanilla bean, seeds scraped
200 g (7 oz) icing (confectioners') sugar

Put the chocolate in a heatproof bowl. Put the butter, milk, glucose and vanilla bean seeds in a saucepan over low heat and cook until the butter is melted. Pour the hot mixture over the chocolate, whisking until combined and the chocolate is melted. Add the icing sugar and continue whisking until fully incorporated. Immediately dip the cooled doughnuts in the chocolate topping so just the top of the doughnut is covered and let them sit for 20 minutes for the topping to set.

*Choux Puffs with Lime
Coconut Filling* PAGE 174

CHOUX PUFFS WITH LIME COCONUT FILLING

MAKES: 18 DIFFICULTY: 🟫🟫

Try something new with the luscious and tropical flavours of these choux puffs. If you like, forgo the meringue and just fill the choux puffs from the base with the lime coconut filling.

CHOUX PASTRY

Prepare one batch of choux pastry dough, following the recipe on page 156.

Preheat the oven to 130°C (250°F) and grease a baking tray with a small amount of butter or vegetable oil spray. Dust the tray lightly with flour.

Put the prepared choux pastry in a piping (icing) bag with a 1.5 cm (⅝ inch) star-shaped nozzle. Pipe the choux pastry into 3.5 cm (1¼ inch) round shapes, approximately 4 cm (1½ inches) apart on the tray. If you have any peaks in your piping, dip your finger in water and tap them down as you go. (You can freeze the choux puffs before baking for up to 1 month.)

Place all the piped choux puffs into the oven at the same time if possible. Bake for 15 minutes then increase the temperature to 150°C (300°F) and cook for a further 15 minutes. Increase the temperature to 170°C (325°F) and cook for a further 12–15 minutes or until the pastry is firm and a dark golden brown on the outside. Do not open the oven door during the baking process. Once the puffs are baked, open the oven door to release the steam and leave them in the oven to continue to dry them out for a few minutes.

LIME COCONUT FILLING

10 g (⅜ oz) custard powder
40 g (1½ oz) caster (superfine) sugar
75 g (2¾ oz/about 4) egg yolks
165 ml (5½ fl oz) coconut cream
25 ml (¾ fl oz) lime juice
1 vanilla bean, seeds scraped
20 g (¾ oz) good-quality white
  chocolate, coarsely chopped
30 g (1 oz) unsalted butter, diced

Whisk together the custard powder and sugar in a heatproof bowl then whisk in the egg yolks. Put the coconut cream, lime juice and vanilla bean seeds in a saucepan over medium heat and bring to the boil. Pour the hot mixture over the egg mixture and whisk together in the bowl before returning the mixture to the saucepan and whisking over medium heat until it comes back to the boil. Remove the pan from the heat and transfer the mixture to a bowl. Add the chocolate, a little at a time, and whisk vigorously to combine and until the chocolate is melted. Whisk the butter into the custard by hand, a piece at a time. (This process can also be done using an electric mixer with a paddle attachment.) Once all the butter is added, press a piece of plastic wrap onto the surface of the custard and place it in the refrigerator to cool for approximately 1 hour. This lime coconut filling can be stored for up to 3 days in the refrigerator prior to use.

MERINGUE

100 g (3½ oz/about 4) egg whites
½ teaspoon cream of tartar
225 g (8 oz) caster (superfine) sugar

It is best to have the choux puffs filled with the lime coconut filling before you start the meringue.

Put the eggs whites, cream of tartar and sugar in a mixing bowl that will fit snugly over a saucepan of water. (If you are using an electric mixer, use the bowl from the mixer.) Half-fill a saucepan with water, place it over medium heat and bring to the boil. Once the water is boiling, remove the pan from the heat and sit the mixing bowl with the egg whites on top. Whisk lightly by hand until the mixture becomes warm to the touch. Transfer the bowl to an electric mixer with a whisk attachment and beat on high speed until medium peaks form. Use as soon as possible after whisking, If the meringue is rigid and difficult to pipe, give it a quick whisk by hand to soften it up again.

ASSEMBLY

Take the baked choux puffs and, using a serrated knife, cut the tops off to leave a small hole. Place the lime coconut filling in a piping (icing) bag with a 1 cm (½ inch) plain nozzle. Fill each choux puff until it is level with the top, cleaning off any excess. (You can also use a spoon to fill the choux puffs.)

Put the meringue in a piping (icing) bag with a 1.2 cm (7/16 inch) star-shaped nozzle. Swirl the meringue in a circular motion on top of the choux puffs. If desired, you can brown the meringue with a small blowtorch. These are best eaten the same day.

SIENA PANFORTE

SERVES: 10-12 DIFFICULTY: 🍫

Siena panforte is an Italian speciality dating back centuries. I like to give it as a gift or share it with my family at Christmas time. If it's overcooked it can be a little dry to eat. Any of the fruit and nuts in the recipe are interchangeable.

130 g (4½ oz) blanched whole almonds
65 g (2¼ oz/⅔ cup) pecans
190 g (6¾ oz) honey
150 g (5½ oz/1 cup) coarsely chopped
  good-quality dark chocolate
  (54% cocoa solids)
70 g (2½ oz) unsalted butter
65 g (2¼ oz) caster (superfine) sugar
65 g (2¼ oz) dried figs
25 g (1 oz) glacé apricots
20 g (¾ oz) glacé cherries
175 g (6 oz) plain (all-purpose) flour
25 g (1 oz) Dutch-process cocoa powder
1 teaspoon ground cinnamon
icing (confectioners') sugar, for dusting

Preheat the oven to 160°C (315°F) and line a baking tray with baking paper. Put the almonds and pecans on the tray and roast for 12–15 minutes, until the almonds are golden brown. Leave the nuts at room temperature to cool.

Increase the oven temperature to 170°C (325°F). Melt the honey, chocolate, butter and sugar together in a plastic bowl in the microwave or in a saucepan over low heat until completely melted. Cool slightly. Fold through the fruits, roasted nuts and dry ingredients, except the icing sugar, using a spatula until just combined.

Grease or line a shallow 20 cm (8 inch) cake ring or tin placed on a baking tray lined with a non-stick mat or baking paper. Wet your hands slightly then pick up the panforte mixture in small handfuls and press it evenly into the prepared cake ring. Wet your hands each time you pick up the mixture to ensure it doesn't stick. Bake for approximately 8 minutes or until it feels quite light and spongy to the touch. Remove from the oven and leave to cool at room temperature in the ring or tin. Once cool, remove from the ring or tin, dust lightly with icing sugar and wrap in cellophane for a gift or cover in plastic wrap and put in an airtight container until ready to use. Siena panforte has a long shelf life and can be kept at room temperature, well-sealed, for up to 3 months.

CHOCOLATE COFFEE ÉCLAIR

MAKES: 9 **DIFFICULTY:** ■■

Coffee and chocolate is a match made in heaven. If my husband, Michael, had his way my next book would be a coffee-flavoured patisserie book. These éclairs are best eaten the same day they are assembled. They will still taste great for up to four days if stored in the refrigerator, but the pastry will become soggy.

CHOUX PASTRY

Prepare one batch of choux pastry dough, following the recipe on page 156.

Preheat the oven to 170°C (325°F) and grease a baking tray with a small amount of butter or vegetable oil spray. Dust the tray lightly with flour and, using your finger or a plastic scraper, mark where you will pipe your éclairs, 10 cm (4 inches) in length, leaving a 5 cm (2 inch) gap between them.

Put the prepared choux pastry in a piping (icing) bag with a 1.5 cm (⅝ inch) star-shaped nozzle. Pipe the choux pastry into straight lines onto the tray, following your guidelines. If it is easier, cut the choux pastry with scissors or a small sharp knife into 10 cm (4 inch) lengths. (You can freeze the éclairs before baking for up to 1 month.)

Place all the piped éclairs in the oven at the same time if possible. While baking, do not open the oven door. Bake for 10 minutes then reduce the temperature to 150°C (300°F) and bake for a further 15 minutes. Reduce the oven temperature to 130°C (250°F) and bake for a further 20 minutes or until the éclairs are firm and a dark golden brown on the outside. Once the éclairs are baked, open the door to release the steam and leave them in the oven to continue to dry out for a few minutes. ☛

COFFEE CUSTARD

100 g (3½ oz/⅔ cup) coarsely chopped
good-quality milk chocolate
35 g (1¼ oz) caster (superfine) sugar
10 g (⅜ oz) custard powder
75 g (2¾ oz/about 4) egg yolks
50 ml (1¾ fl oz) espresso coffee
110 ml (3¾ fl oz) milk
1 vanilla bean, seeds scraped
100 g (3½ oz) unsalted butter, diced

Put the chocolate in a heatproof bowl. Whisk together the sugar and custard powder in a separate heatproof bowl then whisk in the egg yolks, followed by the espresso. Put the milk and vanilla bean seeds in a saucepan over medium heat and bring to the boil. Pour the hot mixture over the egg mixture and whisk together before returning the mixture to the saucepan over medium heat and whisking until it comes back to the boil. Pour the hot mixture over the chocolate and whisk vigorously to combine and until the chocolate is melted. Whisk the butter into the custard by hand, one piece at a time. (This process can also be done using an electric mixer with a paddle attachment.) Once all the butter is added, press a piece of plastic wrap onto the surface of the custard and place it in the refrigerator to cool for approximately 1 hour. This custard can be stored for up to 3 days in the refrigerator prior to use.

CHOCOLATE GLAZE

10 g (⅜ oz) gold-strength gelatine sheets
or 15 g (½ oz) gelatine powder
110 ml (3¾ fl oz) cream (35% fat)
165 g (5¾ oz/¾ cup) caster (superfine)
sugar
55 g (2 oz/½ cup) Dutch-process cocoa
powder, sifted

Soak the gelatine sheets in a bowl of iced water and, once pliable, gently squeeze the sheets to remove any excess water. Set the sheets aside and leave at room temperature. If using the powder, sprinkle it over a bowl containing 30 ml (1 fl oz/1½ tablespoons) cold water. Leave at room temperature until needed.

Put the cream and sugar in a medium saucepan over medium heat and bring to the boil while gently whisking. Add the cocoa powder and bring back to the boil, whisking, then turn off the heat. Combine the mixture with a hand-held blender (or mix vigorously with a hand whisk). Add the gelatine and continue mixing until it is dissolved. Strain the glaze through a fine sieve and cool until it reaches just below body temperature (approximately 35°C/95°F). It is best to sieve the glaze into a plastic bowl as this will enable you to reheat the glaze later in the microwave.

small block of white chocolate

Using a straight-bladed knife, scrape it along the base of the chocolate block to create small shavings.

Place two small holes in the base of each éclair, one at each end, with a plain round piping (icing) nozzle any size between 8 and 10 mm (⅜ and ½ inch). Attach that same piping nozzle to a piping bag. Fill the bag with the coffee custard and pipe it into both holes until the éclair is filled.

Ensure the glaze is at the correct temperature and dip each éclair by holding onto the side horizontally, keeping your fingers closer to the base. Dip the top of each éclair in the prepared glaze and place, glaze side up, on a serving plate. Garnish each éclair with the prepared chocolate shavings. These éclairs are best eaten the same day they are made — they will last up to 3 days but the pastry will go soft.

1. *Place a hole in the base of the éclairs for filling.*

2. *Fill the éclairs with the coffee custard.*

3. *Glaze the top of the éclairs.*

6.

MOUSSE CAKES & CUPS

WHITE CHOCOLATE & PINEAPPLE MOUSSE CUPS

SERVES: 8 DIFFICULTY: ◆ **GLUTEN-FREE**

The summery flavour of pineapple combines beautifully with white chocolate in this dessert, which has been rigorously tested by my son Charlie! If you like, replace the pineapple with layers of fresh berries.

SAUTÉED PINEAPPLE

1 fresh pineapple or 880 g (1 lb 15 oz) tinned pineapple pieces in natural juice
120 g (4¼ oz) soft brown sugar
1 teaspoon vanilla bean paste
10 g (⅜ oz) unsalted butter

Peel the pineapple and cut it into quarters lengthways. Remove the core and dice the pineapple into 1 cm (½ inch) cubes. If using tinned pineapple, drain it well then dice. Put the pineapple, brown sugar, vanilla bean paste and butter in a saucepan over medium heat and gently stir just until the pineapple becomes tender but still holds its shape. Transfer the cooked pineapple to a sieve for a minute to remove the excess juice. Put the pineapple in a sealed container in the refrigerator until required. This can be made up to 3 days in advance and stored in the refrigerator.

WHITE CHOCOLATE MOUSSE

280 g (10 oz) shaved coconut
360 g (12¾ oz) good-quality white chocolate, coarsely chopped
300 ml (10½ fl oz) cream (35% fat) (a)
280 ml (9½ fl oz) cream (35% fat) (b)

Preheat the oven to 160°C (315°F). Spread the coconut out on a baking tray and toast in the oven for 6–8 minutes until golden brown. Set aside to cool at room temperature.

Put the white chocolate in a heatproof bowl. Put the cream (a) in a saucepan over medium heat and bring to the boil. Pour the hot cream over the chocolate, whisking by hand to melt the chocolate and create a ganache. Set aside to cool slightly.

Using an electric mixer with a whisk attachment, whisk the cream (b) on high speed to a semi-whipped consistency (see page 16), then fold through the cooled white chocolate ganache using a spatula until completely combined.

Divide half the pineapple pieces between eight glasses. Set the rest of the pineapple aside for later. Pipe white chocolate mousse halfway up each glass (or use a spoon). Place the glasses in the fridge for 30 minutes to 1 hour. Divide most of the remaining pineapple between the glasses to sit on top of the chilled mousse, and finish with the remaining room-temperature mousse. Sprinkle the toasted coconut and scatter a few pieces of pineapple on top of the mousse and set the glasses aside in the refrigerator for at least 2 hours before serving. This can be made up to 2 days in advance and stored in the refrigerator.

CONCORDE

SERVES: 8-12   **DIFFICULTY:** ◆   GLUTEN-FREE

*Concorde is a French classic that couldn't be overlooked when creating
a chocolate book. The meringue will soften after coming in contact with
the mousse, so eat the concorde close to assembly if you want to enjoy
the crunchy meringue contrasting with the creamy mousse. Otherwise,
you can store it in the refrigerator for up to four days enjoying a softer,
more fudgy texture the longer you store it.*

CHOCOLATE MERINGUE

55 g (2 oz/½ cup) Dutch-process cocoa
  powder
230 g (8 oz) icing (confectioners') sugar
200 g (7 oz/about 8) egg whites
pinch of cream of tartar
230 g (8 oz) caster (superfine) sugar

Sift the cocoa powder and icing sugar together.

Using an electric mixer with a whisk attachment, whisk the egg whites and
cream of tartar to medium peaks and gradually add the caster sugar. Once all
the sugar is added, continue whisking for 1 minute so all the sugar dissolves.
Using a spatula, gently fold through the cocoa powder and icing sugar mixture.
Stop folding once all the dry ingredients are incorporated. Transfer just over
half to a piping (icing) bag with a 1 cm (½ inch) plain nozzle.

Preheat the oven to 140°C (275°F). You will need a baking tray and also a piece
of baking paper cut to the same size. Trace three 16 cm (6¼ inch) circles onto
the paper. Turn the paper over and pipe the meringue into 3 discs, spiralling
from the centre outwards, following your guidelines. (The meringue can also be
spread out evenly with a spoon or spatula.)

Line a separate baking tray with baking paper. Put the remaining meringue in a
piping bag with an 8 mm (⅜ inch) plain nozzle. Pipe individual lines the length
of the tray approximately 1 cm (½ inch) apart on the tray. (You can also spoon
small amounts onto the tray – approximately ½ teaspoon at a time.) Bake both
trays of meringue for approximately 1 hour or until the meringue is crunchy –
the discs may need 10 minutes extra. Cool the meringue at room temperature.
You can make the meringue up to a week in advance and either wrap it securely
with plastic wrap or store in an airtight container until required.

CHOCOLATE MOUSSE

255 g (9 oz) good-quality dark chocolate, coarsely chopped
150 ml (5 fl oz) cream (35% fat) (a)
20 g (¾ oz) unsalted butter, softened
230 ml (7¾ fl oz) cream (35% fat) (b)

Put the chocolate in a heatproof bowl. Put the cream (a) in a saucepan over medium heat and bring to the boil. Pour it over the chocolate, whisking by hand until the chocolate is melted and combined. Add the butter and whisk again until incorporated to create a ganache. Leave the ganache at room temperature until cooled to body temperature.

Using an electric mixer with a whisk attachment, whisk the cream (b) to a semi-whipped consistency (see page 16) and set it aside in the refrigerator until the ganache cools down. Once the ganache is ready, fold through the chilled, semi-whipped cream.

1. *Pipe the chocolate meringue into a disc.*

2. *Pipe the remaining meringue into lines.*

3. *Assemble the chocolate mousse and discs.*

ASSEMBLY

Place a small drop of chocolate mousse onto the plate you are going to serve your cake on and secure one of the meringue discs onto it – ensure you have a large enough plate and keep in mind that once you finish assembling the cake it will be 5–6 cm (2–2½ inches) wider than the meringue base. Place the prepared chocolate mousse in a piping bag with a 1 cm (½ inch) plain nozzle. Pipe a layer of chocolate mousse onto the meringue disc in a spiral – or you can spread the mousse on with a spoon or palette knife. Secure the second disc of meringue directly on top. Cover the disc with another layer of chocolate mousse and the last disc of meringue. Pipe chocolate mousse around the outside of the prepared cake in a thin layer with slightly more mousse on the top. Break the meringue sticks into short lengths and apply them randomly to the side of the cake. Fill the top of the cake with meringue sticks standing upright, broken at various lengths.

Concorde PAGE 186

COCONUT LEMON CHOCOLATE CUPS

MAKES: 8 DIFFICULTY: 🍫

If you like, you can make this incredible dessert up to 5 hours in advance. Replace the lemon juice in the lemon jelly with any citrus fruit juice or passionfruit juice if you like – but only use fresh juice. With this recipe make the jelly first followed by the coconut shortbread cubes, ensuring the jelly is set before you start making the mousse.

LEMON JELLY

5 g (³/₁₆ oz) gold-strength gelatine sheets or 8 g (¼ oz) gelatine powder
110 ml (3¾ fl oz) lemon juice
90 g (3¼ oz) caster (superfine) sugar

Soak the gelatine sheets in a bowl of iced water and, once pliable, gently squeeze the sheets to remove any excess water. Set the sheets aside and leave at room temperature. If using the powder, sprinkle it over a bowl containing 30 ml (1 fl oz/1½ tablespoons) cold water. Leave at room temperature until needed.

Put the lemon juice and sugar in a small saucepan over medium heat and bring to the boil. Cook until the sugar is dissolved. Remove the pan from the heat and add the gelatine, stirring until it dissolves. Pour the mixture into a pitcher and divide it between eight glasses. Place in the refrigerator for 1–2 hours to set.

COCONUT SHORTBREAD CUBES

90 g (3¼ oz) unsalted butter
60 g (2¼ oz/½ cup) icing (confectioners') sugar
90 g (3¼ oz/1 cup) desiccated (shredded) coconut
30 g (1 oz/about ½) whole egg
15 g (½ oz/1½ tablespoons) cornflour (cornstarch)
100 g (3½ oz/⅔ cup) plain (all-purpose) flour
¼ teaspoon baking powder
¼ teaspoon salt

Using an electric mixer with a paddle attachment, beat the butter on medium speed until it is a thick, smooth paste. Sift in the icing sugar and add the coconut and egg. Mix to combine then add the cornflour, plain flour, baking powder and finally the salt. Mix until a dough forms. Press the dough into an even, flat square, wrap it in plastic wrap and place it in the refrigerator to rest for 1 hour, or until firm.

Preheat the oven to 160°C (315°F) and line a baking tray with a non-stick mat or baking paper. Press the prepared shortbread through a cake cooling rack with grids. Cut the shortbread off as it comes out the other side of the grid to create individual cubes. (Alternatively, roll out the shortbread to a 1 cm/½ inch thickness and place back in the fridge before cutting into 1 cm/½ inch cubes.) Place the cubes on the lined tray and bake for 6–8 minutes until golden brown. Set aside in an airtight container – these can be made up to 10 days in advance.

350 ml (12 fl oz) cream (35% fat) (a)

5 g (³⁄₁₆ oz) gold-strength gelatine sheets
or 7 g (¼ oz) gelatine powder

350 g (12 oz/2⅓ cups) coarsely chopped
good-quality milk chocolate

80 ml (2½ fl oz/⅓ cup) cream
(35% fat) (b)

160 ml (5¼ fl oz) coconut cream

zest of 2 lemons

80 ml (2½ fl oz/⅓ cup) lemon juice

Using an electric mixer with a whisk attachment, whisk the cream (a) to a semi-whipped consistency (see page 16). Set aside in the refrigerator.

Soak the gelatine sheets in a bowl of iced water and, once pliable, gently squeeze the sheets to remove any excess water. Set the sheets aside and leave at room temperature. If using the powder, sprinkle it over a bowl containing 20 ml (½ fl oz/1 tablespoon) cold water. Leave at room temperature until needed.

Put the chocolate in a heatproof bowl. Put the cream (b), coconut cream and lemon zest in a saucepan over medium heat and bring to the boil. Add the soaked gelatine and stir to dissolve. Pour the hot mixture over the chocolate, whisking until combined to create a ganache.

Put the lemon juice in a clean saucepan over medium heat and bring to the boil. Pour the hot juice over the chocolate ganache and whisk to combine. Gently fold through the semi-whipped cream with a flexible spatula. Leave at room temperature and use as soon as possible.

Take half the mousse and put it in a piping (icing) bag with a 1 cm (½ inch) plain nozzle then pipe it (or spoon it) on top of the set jelly. Cover with half of the shortbread cubes. Divide the remaining mousse among the eight glasses. Put the glasses back in the refrigerator for 2 hours to set before serving. You can make this 24 hours in advance. It can be eaten after this point, but the shortbread won't have the same crunch. Garnish with the remaining shortbread cubes just before serving.

COFFEE MILK CHOCOLATE CAKE

SERVES: 10-12   DIFFICULTY: 🍫🍫

*Layering a cake is an artform in itself so why not showcase the layers
by leaving them exposed, giving a tantalising glimpse of what's inside?
This cake is best cut with a straight-bladed knife warmed with some
hot water and cleaned and warmed in between each slice.*

COFFEE SPONGE

290 g (10¼ oz/about 5) whole eggs
140 g (5 oz) caster (superfine) sugar
30 g (1 oz) instant coffee powder
140 g (5 oz) plain (all-purpose) flour,
  sifted
pinch of salt
30 g (1 oz) unsalted butter, melted
icing (confectioners') sugar, for dusting

Preheat the oven to 165°C (320°F) and grease four 18 cm (7 inch) round cake
tins. If you don't have the tins, you can prepare two baking tins with sides
that are at least 20 cm (8 inches) wide and long. Spray the tins or trays with
vegetable spray and line them with baking paper.

Using an electric mixer with a whisk attachment, beat the eggs, caster sugar
and coffee on high speed until light, creamy and well aerated. Fold through the
sifted flour and salt gently by hand with a spatula.

Put the melted butter in a bowl, add a little bit of the sponge mixture to it and
combine before folding it all back into the sponge mixture. Divide the sponge
into four portions and fill each cake tin, or divide it in half and pour it into the
trays. Dust lightly with icing sugar. Bake for 10–12 minutes, until they bounce
back when touched. Leave to cool in the tins at room temperature. ☛

1. *Spread equal layers of chocolate mousse onto each sponge.*

2. *Once assembled, coat the cake in the remaining mousse.*

3. *Use a palette knife to create an even finish and to leave the sides of the sponge layers exposed.*

MILK CHOCOLATE MOUSSE

6 g (³⁄₁₆ oz) gold-strength gelatine sheets
  or 9 g (⁵⁄₁₆ oz) gelatine powder
350 g (12 oz/2⅓ cups) coarsely chopped
  good-quality milk chocolate
100 g (3½ oz/about 5) egg yolks
160 g (5½ oz) caster (superfine) sugar
200 ml (7 fl oz) cream (35% fat) (a)
300 ml (10½ fl oz) cream (35% fat) (b)

Soak the gelatine sheets in a bowl of iced water and, once pliable, gently squeeze the sheets to remove any excess water. Set the sheets aside and leave at room temperature. If using the powder, sprinkle it over a bowl containing 30 ml (1 fl oz/1½ tablespoons) cold water. Leave at room temperature until needed.

Put the chocolate in a heatproof bowl. In another heatproof bowl, whisk the egg yolks and sugar until combined. Put the cream (a) in a saucepan over medium heat and bring to the boil. Pour the hot cream over the egg yolk mixture while whisking. Pour the mixture back into the saucepan over low heat, stirring with a heatproof spatula. Heat to 82°C (180°F) to create an anglaise. (If you don't have a sugar thermometer, dip a wooden spoon in the mixture, lift it out and draw a line through the mixture on the spoon with your finger. If the anglaise runs straight over the line, it's not ready. If the line holds without any drips, it's ready. Do this process quickly before the anglaise runs off the spoon.) Add the gelatine and stir until the gelatine is dissolved. Strain the mixture immediately over the chocolate, whisking by hand until the chocolate is melted.

Using an electric mixer with a whisk attachment, whisk the cream (b) to a semi-whipped consistency (see page 16). Fold the cream through the chocolate base with a spatula. Once combined, stop mixing. Place the mousse in the refrigerator for approximately 30 minutes until it has more body, so the layers will hold on the cake.

CHOCOLATE CURLS

300 g (10½ oz/2 cups) coarsely chopped good-quality milk chocolate

Temper the chocolate (see pages 12–14). Spread a small amount of the chocolate in a thin layer on a clean work surface – granite, marble or artificial stone makes the best surface. As soon as the chocolate sets, immediately scrape the chocolate in a circular motion to create curls using a metal scraper or a straight-bladed knife.

ASSEMBLY

icing (confectioners') sugar, for dusting
red fruits, for serving

Remove the sponges from the tins and rub the top surface of each sponge with a serrated knife to remove any loose crust. If you used the two trays, cut out four 18 cm (7 inch) discs. Place one of the sponge discs on a flat tray or display plate. Place a quarter of the milk chocolate mousse on the sponge and spread it over evenly using a palette knife. Place the second sponge on top and ensure that it is level. Place another quarter of the mousse onto the sponge and spread it evenly. Repeat the process. With a palette knife, spread the remaining mousse over the top and outside of the prepared cake – this process is easier with a cake turntable. Spread the mousse as evenly as possible, scraping the excess mousse off with a palette knife to expose the sponge layers around the sides. Place the cake in the refrigerator for approximately 1–2 hours so the mousse firms up. Place the prepared curls on top of the cake just prior to serving, dust with sifted icing sugar and decorate with red fruits.

4. *Work the chocolate on a work surface with a palette knife.*

5. *As soon as the chocolate sets, scrape curls using a metal scraper.*

CHOCOLATE TRUFFLE CAKE

SERVES: 16-18 DIFFICULTY: 🔲🔲 GLUTEN-FREE

If you love a decadent and rich cake, this is a perfect one for you to indulge in. Only a thin sliver is needed for the ultimate chocolate fix.

CHOCOLATE SPONGE

200 g (7 oz/about 10) egg yolks
120 g (4¼ oz) caster (superfine) sugar
100 g (3½ oz) butter, softened
135 g (4¾ oz) good-quality dark chocolate, coarsely chopped
70 g (2½ oz) cornflour (cornstarch)

Preheat the oven to 170°C (325°F). Prepare a 22 cm (8½ inch) cake ring or tin (see page 16). Using an electric mixer with a whisk attachment, beat the egg yolks and sugar on high speed, until light and fluffy.

Melt the butter and chocolate together in a double boiler or in a plastic bowl in the microwave (see page 12). Fold the chocolate and butter mixture through the egg yolk mixture with a spatula. Sift in the cornflour and mix to combine by hand with the spatula. Pour the mixture into the lined cake ring, placed on a flat baking tray. Bake for 20–22 minutes. When it is cooked, the surface of the sponge should bounce back when touched. Remove the cake from the oven and leave to cool in the tin for a few minutes before turning out onto a wire rack to cool completely. Once the sponge is cool, place it in the freezer for approximately 40 minutes – this will make it easier to cut.

Remove the sponge from the freezer and ensure it is right side up. If necessary, use a serrated knife to trim the top of the sponge to make it level. Using a ruler, divide the sponge horizontally into three equal portions and mark around the sponge. Using a serrated knife, carefully cut the three equal layers of sponge, using your marks as a guide. Wrap the sponge in plastic wrap to ensure it doesn't go stale. If not using the sponge straight away, store it in the freezer for up to 2 weeks. 👉

1. Cut the sponge cake into three equal layers.

2. Brush a sponge cake layer with soaking syrup.

3. Alternate layers of mousse with soaked sponge.

SOAKING SYRUP

70 g (2½ oz) caster (superfine) sugar
15 ml (½ fl oz/3 teaspoons) hazelnut liqueur

Put the sugar and 50 ml (1¾ fl oz) water in a saucepan over medium heat and boil until the sugar is dissolved. Remove the pan from the heat and, once cool, add the hazelnut liqueur. This syrup can be made in advance and stored in the refrigerator in an airtight container for up to 2 weeks.

CHOCOLATE MOUSSE

565 ml (19¼ fl oz) cream (35% fat)
485 g (1 lb 1 oz) good-quality dark chocolate, coarsely chopped
90 g (3¼ oz) caster (superfine) sugar
80 g (2¾ oz/¼ cup) liquid glucose
35 ml (1¼ fl oz) hazelnut liqueur

Using an electric mixer with a whisk attachment, whisk the cream to a semi-whipped consistency (see page 16). Set aside in the refrigerator.

Put the chocolate in a heatproof bowl. Put the sugar, 105 ml (3½ fl oz) water and the glucose in a saucepan over medium heat and boil until the sugar is dissolved. Pour the hot mixture over the chocolate, whisking by hand until combined. Add the hazelnut liqueur and whisk to combine. Fold through the semi-whipped cream with a spatula. Use the mousse as soon as the mixing is complete.

Dutch-process cocoa powder, for dusting

Place 1 sponge disc on a baking paper lined tray and place a 22 cm (8½ inch) cake ring around it. Brush it with the prepared syrup and then fill the ring one-third of the way up with chocolate mousse. Spread the chocolate mousse up the sides of the ring, then repeat the process with the two remaining sponge layers. Place a final layer of chocolate mousse on top and level it with a palette knife. Using a dessertspoon, take a large scoop of the remaining mousse and drape it on the top of the cake to create a raised texture on the surface. Repeat the process to create a decoration on top of the cake. Place the cake in the freezer for approximately 4 hours.

Dust the top of the cake lightly with cocoa powder then remove the ring from the cake and carefully transfer the cake to a serving plate. Use a hot, clean knife to cut each slice. While still in the ring, the cake can be frozen for approximately 6 weeks if wrapped. Once defrosted, store in the refrigerator and eat within 4 days.

4. *Level the top of the mousse with a palette knife so it's flat.*

5. *Drizzle chocolate mousse on the top as decoration.*

MILK CHOCOLATE MOUSSE WITH CRUNCHY BASE

SERVES: 10-12   DIFFICULTY: ◆◆◆

Texture, to me, is essential in creating a great cake – and this cake has an abundance of texture, matched with a beautiful flavour, making it divine to eat. It serves 10 to 12 people, or eight if they're really hungry!

FLOURLESS CHOCOLATE SPONGE

40 g (1½ oz) good-quality dark
  chocolate, finely chopped
pinch of salt
85 g (3 oz/about 4) egg yolks
40 g (1½ oz) caster (superfine) sugar (a)
10 g (⅜ oz) Dutch-process cocoa
  powder, sifted
90 g (3¼ oz/about 4) egg whites
pinch of cream of tartar
40 g (1½ oz) caster (superfine) sugar (b)

Preheat the oven to 180°C (350°C). Line two 18 cm (7 inch) cake rings or tins (see page 16). Melt the chocolate and salt together in a double boiler or in a plastic bowl in the microwave (see page 12).

Using an electric mixer with a whisk attachment, beat the egg yolks and caster sugar (a) on high speed for 5 minutes or until white and thick. Gently fold through the cocoa powder and melted chocolate mixture by hand, using a flexible spatula.

In a clean bowl, using the electric mixer with a whisk attachment, beat the egg whites and cream of tartar on high speed until soft to medium peaks form. Gradually add the caster sugar (b) and continue whisking for a minute to enable the sugar to dissolve. Gradually fold the egg white mixture into the egg yolk mixture by hand, using a flexible spatula. Once combined, divide the mixture into the lined cake rings or tins. Bake for 18–20 minutes. To test if the sponges are ready, touch the tops gently and the sponges should spring back. Remove the sponges from the tins and leave to cool on a wire rack. Once cool, rub a serrated knife over the top of the sponges to remove any loose crust.

1. Spread the crispy layer onto the flourless chocolate sponge.

2. Place a layer of mousse over the crispy layer.

3. Spread the mousse up the sides of the cake ring.

CRISPY LAYER

30 g (1 oz) slivered almonds
15 g (½ oz) salted peanuts, chopped
20 g (¾ oz/¾ cup) puffed rice cereal
60 g (2¼ oz) crunchy peanut butter
70 g (2½ oz) good-quality dark chocolate, finely chopped

Preheat the oven to 160°C (315°F) and line a baking tray with baking paper. Put the slivered almonds on the tray and roast for 10–12 minutes, until they are a light golden brown colour. Remove them from the oven and set aside to cool completely. Once cool, roughly chop them. Put the slivered almonds together with the peanuts and puffed rice cereal in a bowl and place the peanut butter on top.

Melt the chocolate in a double boiler or in a plastic bowl in the microwave (see page 12). Add the chocolate to the nuts and peanut butter and stir until all the dry ingredients are coated with the peanut butter and chocolate. Spread this mixture immediately onto the two sponge discs evenly, using a palette knife of the back of a dessertspoon. Leave the sponges at room temperature until required. ☞

4. *Place the remaining mousse on top of the second crispy layer.*

5. *Spread a thin layer of dark chocolate onto bubble wrap.*

6. *Coat the frozen cake with glaze.*

CHOCOLATE RASPBERRY MOUSSE

285 ml (9½ fl oz) cream (35% fat) (a)

90 g (3¼ oz) fresh or frozen raspberries

125 g (4½ oz) good-quality dark chocolate, finely chopped

30 g (1 oz) good-quality milk chocolate, finely chopped

80 g (2¾ oz/about 4) egg yolks

80 g (2¾ oz) caster (superfine) sugar

20 ml (½ fl oz) milk

30 ml (1 fl oz) cream (35% fat) (b)

Place the cream (a) in a bowl with the raspberries and whisk to a semi-whipped consistency (see page 16). Set aside. Put the two chocolates in a separate heatproof bowl.

Whisk the egg yolks and sugar together in another heatproof bowl until combined. Put the milk and cream (b) in a saucepan over medium heat and bring to the boil. Pour the hot mixture over the egg and sugar mixture and whisk to combine. Return the mixture to the saucepan over low heat and cook, stirring continuously, until the temperature reaches 75°C (167°F), to create an anglaise. (If you don't have a sugar thermometer, dip a wooden spoon in the mixture, lift it out and draw a line through the mixture on the spoon with your finger. If the anglaise runs straight over the line, it's not ready. If the line holds without any drips, it's ready. Do this process quickly before the anglaise runs off the spoon.) Immediately strain the mixture over the chocolate, whisking by hand until the chocolate has melted. Fold the semi-whipped cream and raspberry mixture gently through the chocolate mixture using a flexible spatula just until combined. Use the mousse immediately.

CHOCOLATE GLAZE

18 g (⅝ oz) gold-strength gelatine sheets
  or 25 g (1 oz) gelatine powder
175 ml (6 fl oz) cream (35% fat)
260 g (9¼ oz) caster (superfine) sugar
90 g (3¼ oz) Dutch-process cocoa
  powder, sifted

Soak the gelatine sheets in a bowl of iced water and, once pliable, gently squeeze the sheets to remove any excess water. Set the sheets aside and leave at room temperature. If using the powder, sprinkle it over a bowl containing 110 ml (3¾ fl oz) cold water. Leave at room temperature until needed.

Put the cream, sugar and 35 ml (1¼ fl oz) water in a saucepan over medium heat and bring to the boil. Add the cocoa powder and bring to the boil again. Remove the pan from the heat and pour the glaze into a bowl. Process the mixture with a hand-held blender until the glaze is completely combined. Add the gelatine and continue to blend. Strain the mixture into another bowl and place plastic wrap on the surface of the glaze. If using the glaze the same day, leave it at room temperature. Use the glaze at a temperature no higher than 35°C (95°F).

CHOCOLATE HONEYCOMB GARNISH

250 g (9 oz/1⅔ cups) finely chopped
  good-quality dark chocolate
30 cm (12 inch) square piece of clean
  bubble wrap

Temper the chocolate (see pages 12–14). Using a spatula, spread the chocolate onto the bubble side of the bubble wrap so that the bubbles are exposed. Leave the bubble wrap at room temperature to set. If your room temperature is warmer than 25°C (77°F), place in the refrigerator for a short period of time.

ASSEMBLY

Prepare an 18 cm (7 inch) cake ring (see page 16) and line a tray with baking paper. Place one prepared sponge on the lined tray, crispy side up, and place the prepared cake ring around it. Either pipe in the prepared mousse using a piping (icing) bag with a 1 cm (½ inch) plain nozzle, or spoon the mousse in, to reach about halfway up the ring. Use the back of a dessertspoon or a palette knife to wipe the mousse up the sides of the ring (this helps to avoid trapping large air pockets). Place the second sponge on top, crispy side up. Cover the sponge with the remaining mousse. Use a palette knife to level the top of the mousse using your cake ring as a guide. Freeze the cake for a minimum of 4–5 hours before removing the ring. Place the cake back in the freezer until ready for glazing.

To glaze, reheat the glaze if required in the microwave or over a double boiler, and glaze the frozen cake (see page 15). Place the glazed cake directly onto a serving plate. Take the chocolate honeycomb garnishes and poke through any holes that aren't completely open. Place the honeycomb garnish around the side of the cake and a few on top just before serving. This mousse cake will last up to 4 days refrigerated and 1 month in the freezer. Heat the knife before cutting each slice.

Milk Chocolate Mousse with
Crunchy Base PAGE 200

CHERRY BERRY MOUSSE CAKE

SERVES: 10-12 DIFFICULTY: ◆◆◆ **GLUTEN-FREE**

Beautifully presented, this is a cake designed for those who prefer a more subtle chocolate experience as the cherry berry filling cuts down the intensity of the chocolate.

CRISPY CHOCOLATE BASE

45 g (1½ oz) caster (superfine) sugar

100 g (3½ oz) roasted slivered almonds

70 g (2½ oz) good-quality white chocolate, coarsely chopped

20 ml (½ fl oz/1 tablespoon) olive oil

30 g (1 oz) pistachio nuts, chopped

20 g (¾ oz) glacé cherries, chopped

Preheat the oven to 160°C (315°F). Line an 18 x 4.5 cm (7 x 1¾ inch) cake ring (see page 16). Place the prepared cake ring on a flat tray lined with baking paper. Put the sugar and 30 ml (1 fl oz/1½ tablespoons) water in a small saucepan over medium heat and cook just until the sugar is dissolved, to create a sugar syrup.

Put the slivered almonds in a bowl and coat them with the sugar syrup. Transfer them to a baking tray lined with a non-stick mat or baking paper and bake for 12–15 minutes. Stir the almonds every few minutes to ensure they roast evenly. Remove the almonds from the oven when they are a golden brown colour and all the syrup has evaporated. Set aside to cool.

Melt the chocolate in a double boiler or in a plastic bowl in the microwave (see page 12). Transfer the melted chocolate to a bowl with the roasted almonds, olive oil, pistachio nuts and cherries and stir to combine. Pour the mixture immediately into the base of the prepared cake ring. Press it down with the back of a spoon or a palette knife to level it out. Place in the refrigerator for 10–15 minutes to set. Once set, remove from the refrigerator and leave at room temperature.

CHERRY BERRY FILLING

2 g (1⁄16 oz) gold-strength gelatine sheets or 3 g (⅛ oz) gelatine powder

65 g (2¼ oz) glacé cherries

80 g (2¾ oz) desiccated (shredded) coconut

120 g (4¼ oz) frozen or fresh raspberries

15 g (½ oz) caster (superfine) sugar

Soak the gelatine sheets in a bowl of iced water and, once pliable, gently squeeze the sheets to remove any excess water. Set the sheets aside and leave at room temperature. If using the powder, sprinkle it over a bowl containing 30 ml (1 fl oz/1½ tablespoons) cold water. Leave at room temperature until needed.

Place the glacé cherries in a food processor and grind them to a paste, or finely chop them. Transfer to a bowl with the coconut and stir to combine.

1. *Level the crispy chocolate base with a palette knife or the back of a spoon.*

2. *Spread the cherry berry filling over the chocolate base.*

Put the raspberries and caster sugar in a small saucepan over medium heat and bring to the boil then pass the mixture through a sieve to remove the seeds. While the raspberry juice is still warm, add the gelatine and stir it through until it fully dissolves. Combine the prepared raspberry juice with the coconut and cherry mixture then place it directly on top of the crispy chocolate base. Smooth it with the back of a spoon so it is level. Place in the refrigerator for 30 minutes to set. Once set, remove from the refrigerator and leave at room temperature.

MILK CHOCOLATE MOUSSE

270 g (9½ oz) good-quality milk chocolate, finely chopped
45 g (1½ oz/about 2) egg yolks
100 g (3½ oz) caster (superfine) sugar
110 ml (3¾ fl oz) cream (35% fat) (a)
1 vanilla bean, seeds scraped, or
½ teaspoon vanilla bean paste
360 ml (12¼ fl oz) cream (35% fat) (b)

Put the chocolate in a heatproof bowl. In another heatproof bowl, combine the egg yolks and sugar and whisk them by hand until combined. Put the cream (a) and the vanilla bean seeds or paste in a saucepan over medium heat and bring to the boil. Pour the hot cream over the egg yolk mixture and whisk until combined. Return the mixture to the pan over low heat and cook, stirring gently with a heatproof flexible spatula or wooden spoon, until the temperature reaches 80°C (176°F), to create an anglaise. (If you don't have a sugar thermometer, dip a wooden spoon in the mixture, lift it out and draw a line through the mixture on the spoon with your finger. If the anglaise runs straight over the line, it's not ready. If the line holds without any drips, it's ready. Do this process quickly before the anglaise runs off the spoon.) Once the anglaise reaches temperature, remove it from the heat and strain it immediately over the chocolate, whisking until the chocolate is melted. Set aside at room temperature. 👉

Whisk the cream (b) to a semi-whipped consistency (see page 16). Fold the chocolate base through the semi-whipped cream. Place this mousse directly on top of the cherry berry filling, using a piping (icing) bag with a 1 cm (½ inch) plain nozzle (or just use a spoon), to reach halfway up the side of the ring and use a palette knife or dessertspoon to spread it up the sides. Add the remaining mousse and level off the top using a palette knife. Place the finished mousse cake in the freezer for 4–5 hours. Remove the cake ring from your cake and place the cake back into the freezer until you're ready for glazing.

3. *Spread the mousse up the sides of the cake ring.*

4. *Fill to the top with mousse.*

5. *Ensure the top is level.*

6. *Coat the frozen cake with the red glaze.*

7. *Sprinkle coconut onto the chocolate before it sets.*

RED GLAZE

8 g (¼ oz) gold-strength gelatine sheets or 12 g (⁷⁄₁₆ oz) gelatine powder
480 g (1 lb 1 oz) good-quality white chocolate, coarsely chopped
210 ml (7½ fl oz) milk
70 g (2½ oz) liquid glucose
red oil-based powdered food colouring

Soak the gelatine sheets in a bowl of iced water and, once pliable, gently squeeze the sheets to remove any excess water. Set the sheets aside and leave at room temperature. If using the powder, sprinkle it over a bowl containing 30 ml (1 fl oz/1½ tablespoons) cold water. Leave at room temperature until needed.

Melt the chocolate in a double boiler or in a plastic bowl in the microwave (see page 12). Put the milk and glucose in a saucepan over medium heat and bring to the boil. Remove the pan from the heat and add the gelatine, stirring it through until it dissolves. Pour the mixture over the melted white chocolate (in a plastic bowl if you want to reheat it later in the microwave) or a metal bowl (if you will reheat it over a double boiler). Sift in the red colour and mix with a hand-held blender until combined. Press a piece of plastic wrap onto the surface of the glaze and leave it at room temperature to cool to body temperature. Glaze the frozen mousse cake (see page 15). (The remaining glaze is best stored in the freezer until required.)

FINISHING

desiccated (shredded) coconut, for sprinkling
180 g (6½ oz) good-quality white chocolate, coarsely chopped

Place the coconut in a food processor and grind it down to a slightly finer texture. Temper the chocolate (see pages 12–14). Place the chocolate in a paper piping (icing) cone (see page 19) or a zip-lock bag and cut a small amount off the tip of the cone or off the bottom corner of the zip-lock bag with scissors. Pipe round discs of various sizes on a piece of baking paper and, before they set, sprinkle them with the prepared coconut. The discs can be stored prior to use at room temperature (as long as it doesn't exceed 23°C/73°F).

To serve, place the discs on the sides and top of the just glazed cake and store the cake in the refrigerator until ready to serve.

White Chocolate Mousse Cakes with Passionfruit Centres PAGE 212

WHITE CHOCOLATE MOUSSE CAKES WITH PASSIONFRUIT CENTRES

MAKES: 12   DIFFICULTY: ◆◆◆   GLUTEN-FREE

Don't be intimidated by this recipe! All the elements, aside from the mousse, can be made days in advance. For me, passionfruit is the perfect match for white chocolate – cutting through the sweetness and harmonising to create a delicious end result. This is a favourite at many of my family functions. It can be stored in the refrigerator for up to three days or kept in the freezer for a month.

COCONUT DACQUOISE

75 g (2¾ oz/about 3) egg whites

pinch of cream of tartar

25 g (1 oz) caster (superfine) sugar

15 g (½ oz) almond meal

15 g (½ oz/1½ tablespoons) cornflour (cornstarch) or gluten-free plain (all-purpose) flour

35 g (1¼ oz) icing (confectioners') sugar

25 g (1 oz/¼ cup) desiccated (shredded) coconut

Preheat the oven to 170°C (325°F). Using an electric mixer with a whisk attachment, beat the egg whites and cream of tartar on high speed until soft peaks form. Gradually add the sugar while whisking. Add the remaining ingredients and fold them through the meringue.

Take a sheet of baking paper the size of your baking tray and mark twelve 6 cm (2½ inch) circles on it, approximately 2 cm (¾ inch) apart (you may need to use two baking trays). Turn the piece of paper over and place it on the tray. Put the prepared dacquoise into a piping (icing) bag with a 1 cm (½ inch) plain nozzle and pipe it into the circles, spiralling from the centre outwards. (You can also spread this mixture out using a small knife or spoon.) Bake for 12–15 minutes until golden brown. Remove from the oven and leave on the tray to cool at room temperature.

PASSIONFRUIT CREAM

2 g (¹⁄₁₆ oz) gold-strength gelatine sheets
or 3 g (¹⁄₈ oz) gelatine powder

60 ml (2 fl oz/¼ cup) passionfruit juice
(from about 6 passionfruits)

90 g (3¼/about 4½) egg yolks

40 g (1½ oz) caster (superfine) sugar

50 ml (1¾ fl oz) milk

125 ml (4 fl oz/½ cup) cream (35% fat)

Soak the gelatine sheets in a bowl of iced water and, once pliable, gently squeeze the sheets to remove any excess water. Set the sheets aside and leave at room temperature. If using the powder, sprinkle it over a bowl containing 30 ml (1 fl oz/1½ tablespoons) cold water. Leave at room temperature until needed.

To make passionfruit juice, cut open the passionfruits, scoop out the pulp and sieve out the seeds. Measure out 60 ml (2 fl oz/¼ cup). Put the passionfruit juice in a small saucepan over medium heat and bring to the boil. Set aside.

Put the egg yolks and sugar in a heatproof bowl and whisk together to combine. Put the milk and cream in a saucepan over medium heat and bring to the boil. Slowly pour this hot mixture over the egg yolks and sugar, whisking by hand. Once the two mixtures are combined, return the mixture to the saucepan and cook over low heat, stirring constantly with a heatproof spatula, until it reaches 80°C (176°F), to create an anglaise. (If you don't have a sugar thermometer, dip a wooden spoon in the mixture, lift it out and draw a line through the mixture on the spoon with your finger. If the anglaise runs straight over the line, it's not ready. If the line holds without any drips, it's ready. Do this process quickly before the anglaise runs off the spoon.) Add the soaked gelatine and passionfruit juice and stir to combine. Strain the mixture immediately into a 27 x 17 cm (10¾ x 6½ inch) slab tin lined with plastic wrap. Place on a level shelf in the freezer for 1–2 hours or until frozen. Once frozen, cut into individual 3 cm (1¼ inch) squares, then return to the freezer until required. This recipe for passionfruit cream makes more than needed for the mousse cakes. The excess can be stored in the freezer in a sealed container for up to 6 weeks.

WHITE CHOCOLATE MOUSSE

500 ml (17 fl oz/2 cups) cream (35% fat)

5 g (³⁄₁₆ oz) gold-strength gelatine sheets
or 8 g (¼ oz) gelatine powder

85 g (3 oz/about 4) egg yolks

95 g (3¼ oz) caster (superfine) sugar

225 g (8 oz) good-quality white
chocolate, finely chopped

Whisk the cream to a semi-whipped consistency (see page 16). Set it aside in the refrigerator.

Soak the gelatine sheets in a bowl of iced water and, once pliable, gently squeeze the sheets to remove any excess water. Set the sheets aside and leave at room temperature. If using the powder, sprinkle it over a bowl containing 25 ml (¾ fl oz) cold water. Leave at room temperature until needed.

Using an electric mixer with a whisk attachment, beat the egg yolks on high speed until combined. Put the sugar and 40 ml (1¼ fl oz/2 tablespoons) water in a small saucepan over medium heat and heat until it reaches 123°C (253°F). (If you don't have a sugar thermometer, use a teaspoon to take a small amount of the boiled sugar syrup and drop it into a bowl of cold water – if the sugar is ready it will make a firm, pliable ball.) Pour the syrup over the whisked egg yolks and continue to whisk until the mixture reaches room temperature.

Melt the chocolate in a double boiler or in a plastic bowl in the microwave (see page 12). ☞

Melt the gelatine gently until it is completely liquid, either in the microwave on High (100%), in bursts for a few seconds at a time, or over a double boiler. Add a small amount of the egg yolk mixture to the gelatine and mix to combine, then stir it back into the egg yolk mixture.

Fold a quarter of the semi-whipped cream into the melted chocolate. Fold this chocolate mixture through the egg mixture gently, then fold through the remaining cream. Use this mousse immediately once made, before the gelatine sets.

WHITE CHOCOLATE GLAZE

4 g (⅛ oz) gold-strength gelatine sheets or 6 g (³⁄₁₆ oz) gelatine powder
300 g (10½ oz) good-quality white chocolate, coarsely chopped
125 ml (4 fl oz/½ cup) milk
40 g (1½ oz/1½ tablespoons) liquid glucose

Soak the gelatine sheets in a bowl of iced water and, once pliable, gently squeeze the sheets to remove any excess water. Set the sheets aside and leave at room temperature. If using the powder, sprinkle it over a bowl containing 25 ml (¾ fl oz) cold water. Leave at room temperature until needed.

Put the chocolate in a heatproof bowl. Put the milk and glucose in a saucepan over medium heat and bring to the boil. Remove the pan from the heat, add the gelatine and whisk until it is dissolved. Pour the mixture over the chocolate, whisking to combine. Place plastic wrap on the surface and, if using within 4 days, place it in the refrigerator. If storing for a longer period, put the glaze in a sealed container and store it in the freezer for 1 month. The glaze can be made fresh and used once it cools down. When glazing, you need to create more glaze than you require so it covers the sides of the cakes completely. You can store the remaining glaze in the refrigerator for up to a week or in the freezer for up to 1 month.

YELLOW CHOCOLATE GARNISH

120 g (4¼ oz) good-quality white chocolate, finely chopped
yellow oil-based powdered food colouring

Take a piece of baking paper approximately 30 cm (12 inches) square and crumple it up into a tight ball in your hands. Spread it out flat, then crumple it up again before spreading it out as flat as you can. Temper the chocolate (see pages 12–14). Sift in the yellow food colouring and stir to combine. Place the chocolate in a paper piping (icing) cone (see page 19) or a zip-lock bag and cut a small amount off the tip of the cone or off the bottom corner of the zip-lock bag with scissors. Pipe round discs of various sizes on the scrunched baking paper. Leave to set at room temperature (as long as your room temperature is below 25°C/77°F, otherwise refrigerate). Once the yellow discs have set, carefully peel them off the paper and store in an airtight container at room temperature for up to 2 months.

1. *Pipe the dacquoise into small coils.*

2. *Pipe the yellow chocolate garnish.*

3. *Coat the frozen mousse cakes with white chocolate glaze.*

ASSEMBLY

Prepare twelve 7 x 4.5 cm (2¾ x 1¾ inch) cake rings or tins (see page 16). Line a flat tray with baking paper and place the prepared rings on top. Place a disc of dacquoise into each ring then cover with white chocolate mousse, either using a piping (icing) bag with a 1 cm (½ inch) plain nozzle, or a spoon. Spread the mousse up the sides of the prepared rings using the back of a spoon. Place a frozen passionfruit insert inside each ring and cover with the remaining white chocolate mousse. Level the top of the mousse with a spatula. Place the mousse cakes in the freezer for 5–6 hours until firm to the touch. Remove the rings by pushing the cakes gently up through the base. Place the mousse cakes back in the freezer. Glaze the mousse cakes (see page 15), reheating the glaze if required. Place the prepared yellow chocolate garnishes randomly over the outside of each cake. Store in the refrigerator for up to 3 days.

CARAMEL CHOCOLATE MOUSSE CAKE

SERVES: 12 DIFFICULTY: ♦♦♦ GLUTEN-FREE

If you're looking to impress family or friends – this cake is ideal. It's a complex cake, but all the elements can be made well in advance and stored, aside from the mousse.

40 g (1½ oz/¼ cup) hazelnuts

75 g (2¾ oz/about 3) egg whites

pinch of cream of tartar

25 g (1 oz) caster (superfine) sugar

30 g (1 oz/¼ cup) icing (confectioners') sugar, plus extra for dusting

15 g (½ oz/1½ tablespoons) hazelnut meal

HAZELNUT DACQUOISE BASE

Preheat the oven to 160°C (315°F). Put the hazelnuts on a baking tray and roast them for 10–12 minutes until the skins loosen slightly. Remove the hazelnuts from the oven, place them in a tea towel (dish towel) and rub to remove the skins. Roughly chop the hazelnuts and set aside.

Increase the oven temperature to 170°C (325°F). You will need a baking tray at least 32 cm (12¾ inches) square and a piece of baking paper cut to the same size. Trace two 16 cm (6¼ inch) circles onto the paper and turn it over.

Using an electric mixer with a whisk attachment, beat the egg whites and cream of tartar on high speed until soft to medium peaks form. Gradually add the caster sugar and continue to whisk for a minute to allow the sugar to dissolve. Sift in the icing sugar and hazelnut meal and fold them through the meringue gently with a flexible spatula. Transfer the dacquoise mixture to a piping (icing) bag with a 1 cm (½ inch) plain nozzle. Pipe the mixture in coils onto the prepared tray, using your guidelines (or spread it out evenly with the back of a spoon or metal spatula). Sprinkle the discs with the hazelnuts and then dust lightly with icing sugar. Bake for 12–15 minutes until golden brown. Leave on the tray to cool at room temperature. The dacquoise can be made in advance and stored in the freezer for up to 6 weeks if well wrapped. The dacquoise will have a chewy texture and is easy to handle and remove from the tray if frozen. ☞

75 g (2¾ oz/⅓ cup) caster (superfine)
  sugar
25 g (1 oz) salted butter
pinch of salt

Put a clean saucepan over medium heat. Add a small amount of sugar at a time, gently stirring until it is light golden before adding the next lot. Stir until it is all a golden brown colour and the sugar is dissolved. Remove from the heat and immediately add the butter and salt and whisk by hand to combine. Pour onto a sheet of baking paper or a non-stick baking mat on a heatproof work surface. Leave the caramel until it hardens enough to snap, which will only take a few minutes – don't leave the caramel for an extended period of time at room temperature as it will absorb moisture and become tacky. Break the caramel up into smaller pieces. Once cool, place the caramel in a food processor and grind to a powder. This can be stored in an airtight container in the freezer for 3 months.

1. *Pour the caramel out onto baking paper or a baking mat as soon as it is ready.*

2. *Test the caramel crème brûlée centre by running a finger across the spoon – if the line holds, the mixture is ready.*

CARAMEL CRÈME BRÛLÉE CENTRE

2 g (1/16 oz) gold-strength gelatine sheets
  or 3 g (⅛ oz) gelatine powder
50 g (1¾ oz) powdered caramel
  (see caramel recipe above)
50 g (1¾ oz/about 2½) egg yolks
190 ml (6½ fl oz) cream (35% fat)
½ teaspoon vanilla bean paste

Soak the gelatine sheets in a bowl of iced water and, once pliable, gently squeeze the sheets to remove any excess water. Set the sheets aside and leave at room temperature. If using gelatine powder, sprinkle it over a bowl containing 10 ml (¼ fl oz/2 teaspoons) cold water. Leave at room temperature until needed.

Combine the powdered caramel and egg yolks in a heatproof bowl and whisk by hand (there may still be lumps at this stage, they will dissolve as you go). Put the cream and vanilla bean paste in a saucepan over medium heat and bring to the boil. Pour the hot mixture over the egg yolk and caramel mixture and whisk to combine. Return the mixture to the saucepan and stir gently with

3. *Pipe the chocolate garnish using a template as a guide.*

4. *Pour the chocolate mousse on top of the dacquoise.*

5. *Carefully place the frozen crème brûlée centre over the top.*

a heatproof spatula over low heat until the temperature reaches 84°C (183°F), to create an anglaise. (If you don't have a sugar thermometer, dip a wooden spoon in the mixture, lift it out and draw a line through the mixture on the spoon with your finger. If the anglaise runs straight over the line, it's not ready. If the line holds without any drips, it's ready. Do this process quickly before the anglaise runs off the spoon.)

Once the anglaise reaches temperature, immediately strain it into a bowl. Add the gelatine and stir until it is dissolved. Grease a bowl with a 17 cm (6½ inch) or smaller diameter with vegetable oil spray and line with plastic wrap. Pour the prepared mixture into the bowl and freeze for approximately 3 hours or until solid. Keep this in the freezer until you are ready to assemble your cake. This can be made in advance and stored in the freezer, wrapped, for up to 4 weeks.

DUO CHOCOLATE MOUSSE

350 ml (12 fl oz) cream (35% fat)

55 g (2 oz/¼ cup) caster (superfine) sugar

50 g (1¾ oz/about 2½) egg yolks

130 g (4½ oz) good-quality dark chocolate, coarsely chopped

100 g (3½ oz/⅔ cup) coarsely chopped good-quality milk chocolate

Whisk the cream to a semi-whipped consistency (see page 16) then set aside in the refrigerator.

Fill a medium saucepan one-third full with water, place it over medium heat and bring the water to a simmer. In a bowl that fits snugly on top of the saucepan, combine the sugar, 40 ml (1¼ fl oz/2 tablespoons) water and the egg yolks and whisk by hand to combine before placing the bowl over the saucepan of simmering water. Continue whisking until the mixture becomes light and creamy (this may take up to 5 minutes). Remove from the heat.

Melt the chocolates together in a double boiler or in a plastic bowl in the microwave (see page 12). Fold the melted chocolate through the whipped egg yolk by hand with a spatula then fold through the cream until just combined. You must use the mousse immediately. 👉

GLAZE

10 g (⅜ oz) gold-strength gelatine sheets
   or 15 g (½ oz) gelatine powder
120 ml (4 fl oz) cream (35% fat)
50 g (1¾ oz) good-quality white
   chocolate, finely chopped
130 g (4½ oz) caster (superfine) sugar
120 g (4¼ oz) liquid glucose

Soak the gelatine sheets in a bowl of iced water and, once pliable, gently squeeze the sheets to remove any excess water. Set the sheets aside and leave at room temperature. If using the powder, sprinkle it over a bowl containing 30 ml (1 fl oz/1½ tablespoons) cold water. Leave at room temperature until needed.

Put the cream in a small saucepan over medium heat and bring to the boil. Cover and keep warm.

Put the chocolate in a heatproof bowl. Put the sugar in a medium saucepan over low heat, stirring it gently until the sugar is fully dissolved and caramelised and you have achieved a light caramel colour. Remove the pan from the heat and, whisking constantly, add the hot cream immediately to stop the caramel cooking. (Be careful when adding the cream as it will generate a lot of steam and increase in volume very quickly.) Add the glucose and gelatine sheets and continue whisking until the gelatine is dissolved. Pour the hot liquid over the chocolate, whisking vigorously by hand until the chocolate is melted. Place plastic wrap on the surface of the glaze and, if using on the same day, leave at room temperature. Otherwise, store in the refrigerator for up to 1 week or in the freezer for up to 1 month.

YELLOW CHOCOLATE GARNISH

120 g (4¼ oz) good-quality white
   chocolate, finely chopped
yellow oil-based powdered food
   colouring

Temper the chocolate (see pages 12–14). Sift in the yellow food colouring and stir to combine.

Draw an 18 cm (7 inch) circle on a sheet of baking paper and turn it over. (If you can source an acetate sheet for cooking, place it over the drawn disc.) Put the yellow chocolate in a paper piping (icing) cone (see page 19) or a zip-lock bag and cut a small amount off the tip of the cone or off the bottom corner of the zip-lock bag with scissors. Pipe a decorative disc on top of the acetate sheet or directly on top of the baking paper, swirling from the inside out, creating swirls tight enough so that the shape won't break when the disc is set. Leave to set at room temperature for approximately 30 minutes (If your room temperature is above 24°C/75°F, place it in the refrigerator.) Once the yellow disc has set, use a dry, warm knife and trim off any areas that you piped outside the line to neaten the disc. Remove the disc from the plastic or paper only when you are ready to place it on the cake. This disc can be pre-made and stored in an airtight container at room temperature for up to 8 weeks.

ASSEMBLY

Line an 18 x 4.5 cm (7 x 1¾ inch) cake ring (see page 16), and place it on a tray lined with baking paper. Place a disc of hazelnut dacquoise in the centre of the ring. Pour the duo chocolate mousse onto the dacquoise to about halfway up the cake ring. Spread the mousse up the side of the cake ring using the back of a dessertspoon. Place the frozen caramel crème brûlée in the centre of the cake then cover with another layer of chocolate mousse approximately 1 cm (½ inch) in thickness. Place the second disc of hazelnut dacquoise on top of the mousse then cover with the remaining mousse. Level the top of the mousse off to create a flat, even surface using a palette knife. Place the prepared mousse cake straight into the freezer and freeze for 4–6 hours until solid. Remove the cake ring from your cake and place it back in the freezer until you're ready for glazing. Reheat the glaze if required and glaze the frozen mousse cake (see page 15). Place the chocolate garnish directly onto the glazed cake and store in the refrigerator until ready to serve.

6. *Cover with another layer of mousse.*

7. *Place in a second disc of dacquoise.*

8. *Fill with the remaining mousse and even off the top using a palette knife.*

7.
DESSERTS

DARK CHOCOLATE ICE CREAM

MAKES: 1 LITRE (35 FL OZ/4 CUPS)   DIFFICULTY: ◆   GLUTEN-FREE

Making ice cream does require an ice-cream machine. When placing a scoop or quenelle of ice cream onto a plate, always place some crushed roasted nuts underneath to stop it sliding around.

150 g (5½ oz/1 cup) finely chopped good-quality dark chocolate (70% cocoa solids)
160 g (5½ oz/about 8) egg yolks
115 g (4 oz) caster (superfine) sugar
30 g (1 oz/1 tablespoon) honey
225 ml (7½ fl oz) cream (35% fat)
225 ml (7½ fl oz) milk
1 vanilla bean, seeds scraped

Put the chocolate in a large heatproof bowl and prepare an ice bath. Place another bowl, or container, at least 1 litre (35 fl oz/4 cup) capacity in the freezer. In a separate heatproof bowl, whisk the egg yolks, sugar and honey together.

Put the cream, milk and vanilla bean seeds in a saucepan over medium heat and bring to the boil. Pour the hot mixture over the egg yolk mixture and whisk to combine, then return the mixture to the pan over low heat and cook, stirring gently with a spatula or wooden spoon, until the temperature reaches 80°C (176°F), to create an anglaise. (If you don't have a sugar thermometer, dip a wooden spoon in the mixture, lift it out and draw a line through the mixture on the spoon with your finger. If the anglaise runs straight over the line, it's not ready. If the line holds without any drips, it's ready. Do this process quickly before the anglaise runs off the spoon.)

Once the anglaise reaches temperature, remove the pan from the heat and immediately strain the mixture over the chocolate, whisking to combine and until the chocolate is melted. Place the mixture over the ice bath, whisking intermittently until the mixture cools to around 5°C (41°F).

Pour the chilled mixture into an ice-cream machine and churn following the manufacturer's directions. Transfer the ice cream to the chilled container in the freezer. You can store the ice cream for up to 4 weeks in the freezer. It is easiest to scoop with a spoon dipped in hot water.

Garnish with berries and chocolate shavings, if desired.

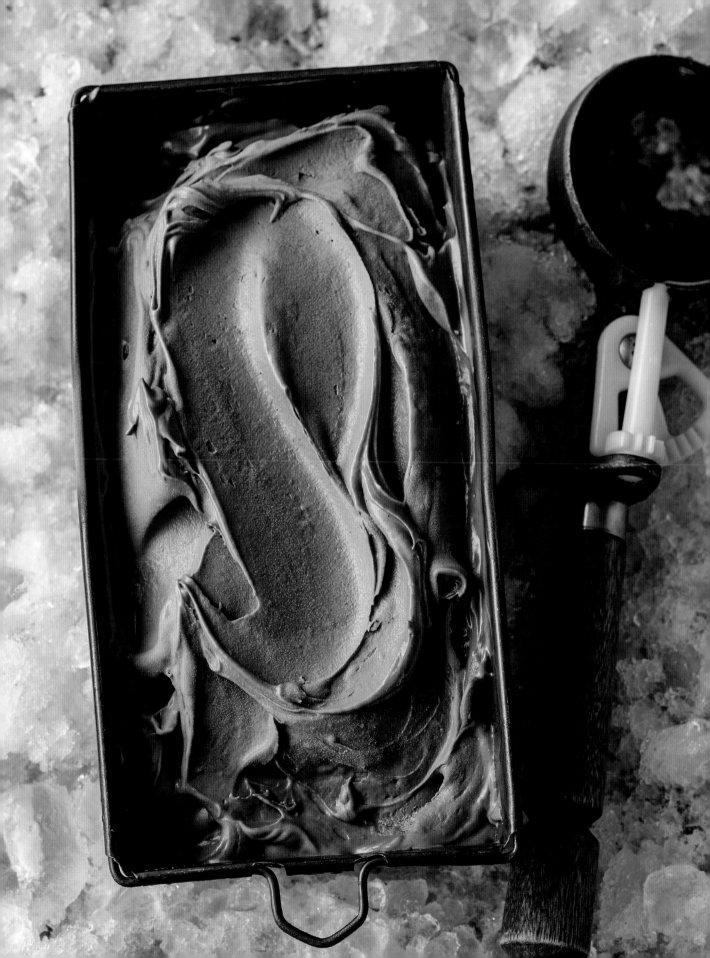

WHITE CHOCOLATE & CHAI CRÈME BRÛLÉES

MAKES: 6 DIFFICULTY: 🍫 GLUTEN-FREE

A modern twist on a French classic, this is a simple dessert that can be made in advance with the final touches added just before serving. It's great on its own or with a piece of crunchy biscotti for dipping.

55 g (2 oz) good-quality white chocolate, finely chopped
290 ml (10 fl oz) cream (35% fat)
1 vanilla bean, seeds scraped
15 g (½ oz) chai tea leaves
135 g (4¾ oz/about 7) egg yolks
90 g (3¼ oz) caster (superfine) sugar (a)
100 g (3½ oz) caster (superfine) sugar (b), for caramelising

Preheat the oven to 140°C (275°F). Put the chocolate in a heatproof bowl. Put the cream and vanilla bean seeds in a saucepan over medium heat and bring to the boil. Remove the pan from the heat, add the tea and leave to steep for 5 minutes. Strain the mixture, then re-measure the cream and top it back up to its original volume of 290 ml (10 fl oz).

In another heatproof bowl, whisk the egg yolks and sugar (a) together by hand until the mixture starts to lighten. Pour the cream mixture over the egg mixture and whisk together. Return everything to the pan over low heat and cook, stirring, until the temperature reaches 80°C (176°F). (If you don't have a sugar thermometer, dip a wooden spoon in the mixture, lift it out and draw a line through the mixture on the spoon with your finger. If the anglaise runs straight over the line, it's not ready. If the line holds without any drips, it's ready. Do this process quickly, before the anglaise runs off the spoon.) Immediately strain the mixture over the chopped white chocolate, whisking to combine.

Divide the mixture evenly into six 8 x 4 cm (3¼ x 1½ inch) ramekins and place them in a large baking dish or tin with sides. Place the dish with the ramekins in the oven and fill it with water so it comes halfway up the sides of the ramekins. Cook for 22–25 minutes. When it's ready, the crème brûlée will be slightly wobbly but set. Remove the ramekins from the water bath and place them in the refrigerator for 2 hours to set completely. These can be made up to 48 hours prior to serving and stored in the refrigerator. To finish, sprinkle the surface with the sugar (b) before caramelising it with a blowtorch. If you don't have a blowtorch, brown them under a grill (broiler) or serve the brûlées as they are.

CHOCOLATE SOUFFLÉS

MAKES: 8 DIFFICULTY:

Creating the perfect soufflé can be a challenge. For me, this soufflé is the ultimate in flavour and texture and isn't too difficult to create. It needs to be served immediately after baking and I like it best with a scoop of chocolate ice cream in the centre.

melted butter, for greasing
icing (confectioners') sugar (a), for
    coating the moulds
35 g (1¼ oz) unsalted butter
40 g (1½ oz) plain (all-purpose) flour
pinch of salt
190 ml (6½ fl oz) milk
35 g (1¼ oz) caster (superfine) sugar (a)
135 g (4¾ oz) good-quality chocolate,
    coarsely chopped (70% cocoa solids)
80 g (2¾ oz/about 4) egg yolks
125 g (4½ oz/about 5) egg whites
½ teaspoon cream of tartar
50 g (1¾ oz) caster (superfine) sugar (b)
icing (confectioners') sugar (b), for
    dusting

Preheat the oven to 170°C (325°F). Prepare eight 8 x 6.5 cm (3¼ x 2½ inch) ramekins or soufflé moulds by brushing melted butter inside the ramekins until evenly coated. Dust the inside of the ramekins with icing sugar (a) and tap out the excess. Place the prepared ramekins on a baking tray.

Mix the butter, flour and salt with your hands until they form a paste, leaving no dry flour. Put the milk and caster sugar (a) in a small saucepan over medium heat and bring to the boil. Reduce the heat to low, add the flour and butter paste to the hot milk and whisk for 3 minutes, or until the paste dissolves and the mixture has a thick, gummy texture. Add the chocolate and egg yolks and stir until melted and combined.

Using an electric mixer with a whisk attachment, beat the egg whites and cream of tartar on medium speed to medium peaks. Gradually add the caster sugar (b) and continue whisking to stiff, glossy peaks. Add one-third of the meringue at a time to the chocolate mixture and gently fold it through by hand with a spatula before adding and incorporating the remainder in two batches.

Once combined, divide the mixture between the eight ramekins by spooning it in to just below the top. Bake the soufflés immediately for 9–10 minutes – the baking time may vary if you use different-sized ramekins. Serve the soufflés as soon they come out of the oven, dusted with icing sugar (b).

MODERN BANANA SPLIT

SERVES: 6 DIFFICULTY: 🍫

An inventive twist on the classic dessert combination of bananas and chocolate. The shortbread cubes can also be replaced with some roasted almonds to create a gluten-free option.

SHORTBREAD CRUMBLE

75 g (2¾ oz) unsalted butter

45 g (1½ oz) icing (confectioners') sugar, sifted

30 g (1 oz/about ½) whole egg

pinch of salt

125 g (4½ oz) plain (all-purpose) flour

Put the butter in the bowl of an electric mixer with a paddle attachment and mix on medium speed until softened and smooth. Add the icing sugar followed by the egg and finally the salt and flour. Mix just until it comes to a crumble consistency without forming a dough.

Preheat the oven to 160°C (315°F) and line a baking tray with a non-stick mat or baking paper.

Spread the crumble mixture onto the prepared tray and bake for 6–7 minutes until golden brown. Set aside in an airtight container – this can be made up to 10 days in advance.

CARAMELISED SLICED BANANAS

3 ripe bananas
90 g (3¼ oz) caster (superfine) sugar

Peel the bananas and slice them on a slight angle approximately 1 cm (½ inch) thick. Put them on a tray lined with baking paper and sprinkle each slice with sugar. Put the banana slices under a grill (broiler) on medium heat until the sugar is melted and caramelised. You can prepare the bananas up to 30 minutes in advance.

CHANTILLY CREAM

240 ml (8 fl oz) cream (35% fat)
½ teaspoon vanilla bean paste
50 g (1¾ oz) caster (superfine) sugar

Put the cream, vanilla bean paste and sugar in a bowl and whisk until the cream holds its shape. You can store the cream in the refrigerator for up to 1 hour before serving.

CHOCOLATE SAUCE

50 g (1¾ oz) good-quality dark
  chocolate, coarsely chopped
100 ml (3½ fl oz) cream (35% fat)

Put the chocolate in a heatproof bowl. Put the cream in a saucepan over medium heat and bring to the boil. Pour the hot cream over the chocolate, whisking by hand until the chocolate is melted. Use the sauce as soon as possible after making it so it doesn't set.

ASSEMBLY

Scatter pieces of the banana onto each plate followed by dollops of chocolate sauce placed onto each plate with a teaspoon. Dip a spoon in hot water and then scoop or quenelle one scoop of the chantilly cream onto each plate. Randomly place an assortment of the shortbread crumble on each plate and serve.

Chocolate Fondants with
Chocolate Chip Ice Cream PAGE 234

CHOCOLATE FONDANTS WITH CHOCOLATE CHIP ICE CREAM

MAKES: 9 DIFFICULTY: 🍫

Chocolate fondants are really simple to make — and so good to eat! I tend to test a pudding to determine the baking time before serving them to my guests. I have accompanied this dessert with a homemade ice cream that requires an ice-cream machine. Alternatively, simply skip this part and serve the fondants with good-quality store-bought ice cream. The ice-cream recipe will give you some leftovers to enjoy.

200 g (7 oz/about 10) egg yolks
215 g (7½ oz) caster (superfine) sugar
550 ml (19 fl oz) cream (35% fat)
2 vanilla beans, seeds scraped
90 g (3¼ oz) good-quality milk
  chocolate chips

CHOCOLATE CHIP ICE CREAM

Place a bowl or container at least 1 litre (35 fl oz/4 cup) capacity in the freezer and prepare an ice bath. In a separate heatproof bowl, whisk the egg yolks and sugar together. Put the cream and vanilla bean seeds in a saucepan over medium heat and bring to the boil. Remove the pan from the heat and pour the hot cream mixture over the egg yolks and sugar, whisking to combine. Return everything to the pan over low heat, stirring gently with a spatula or wooden spoon, until the temperature reaches 82°C (180°F) to create an anglaise. (If you don't have a sugar thermometer, dip a wooden spoon in the mixture, lift it out and draw a line through the mixture on the spoon with your finger. If the anglaise runs straight over the line, it's not ready. If the line holds without any drips, it's ready. Do this process quickly before the anglaise runs off the spoon.)

Once the anglaise reaches temperature, remove the pan from the heat and strain the mixture into a bowl over the ice bath. Whisk the anglaise intermittently until the mixture cools to around 5°C (41°F).

Pour the chilled mixture into an ice-cream machine, add the chocolate chips and churn following the manufacturer's directions. Transfer the ice cream to the chilled container in the freezer. You can store the ice cream for up to 4 weeks in the freezer.

LIQUID CENTRE CHOCOLATE PUDDINGS

125 g (4½ oz) good-quality dark
chocolate, coarsely chopped

20 g (¾ oz/2 tablespoons) Dutch-
process cocoa powder

150 g (5½ oz) unsalted butter

pinch of sea salt

250 g (9 oz/about 4) whole eggs

160 g (5½ oz) caster (superfine) sugar

65 g (2¼ oz) plain (all-purpose) flour,
sifted

Take nine individual 7 x 4 cm (2¾ x 1½ inch) pudding moulds, ramekins or cake rings (individual rings are the easiest to work with or it is best to serve the puddings in the moulds) and spray them lightly with vegetable spray. Line the sides with a strip of baking paper slightly higher than the top of the mould. Place them on a baking tray lined with baking paper.

Melt the dark chocolate, cocoa powder, butter and sea salt together in a double boiler or in a plastic bowl in the microwave (see page 12).

Whisk the eggs with the sugar in a mixing bowl just until combined, fold the chocolate mixture into it and combine by hand with a spatula, followed by the sifted flour. Pour the mixture into the prepared moulds, filling each mould approximately three-quarters full (approximately 80 g/2¾ oz per mould). Place the prepared puddings in the refrigerator for at least 2 hours. They can sit for up to 48 hours in the refrigerator prior to baking.

Preheat the oven to 180°C (350°F). It's best to test one fondant prior to serving to ensure you have a liquid centre. Place one fondant with a small square of baking paper underneath in the oven for 9–10 minutes. Remove the fondant from the oven, remove it from the mould and test the centre. If it is liquid but the sides hold up, this is the correct cooking time and temperature to bake the remaining fondants. Be careful as only a few extra minutes in the oven will mean the fondants are baked solid. Serve the chocolate fondants with the prepared ice cream.

CHOCOLATE PARFAIT WITH STRAWBERRY SAUCE

SERVES: 8   DIFFICULTY: 🍫🍫   **GLUTEN-FREE**

You can't get a much more attractive dessert than this parfait — the spun sugar sets it off and creates an impressive finish. All the elements of this recipe can be made in advance, apart from the spun sugar.

CHOCOLATE PARFAIT

35 g (1¼ oz) caster (superfine) sugar (a), plus extra for the bowl of cones

245 ml (8¼ fl oz) cream (35% fat)

75 g (2¾ oz/about 3) egg whites

pinch of cream of tartar

40 g (1½ oz/about 2) egg yolks

55 g (2 oz/¼ cup) caster (superfine) sugar (b)

105 g (3¾ oz) good-quality dark chocolate, coarsely chopped

For this parfait I have used cones created from baking paper triangles. Cut eight individual paper triangles for each parfait, approximately 32 x 24 x 23 cm (12¾ x 9½ x 9 inches) and roll them into a cone shape, ensuring the tip is closed. Fold the ends of the paper into the cone to secure it. Pour some caster sugar into a bowl big enough to stand the eight cones in, and which will fit in your freezer. Ensure the eight cones are pressed into the sugar and secure to ensure they are stable.

Whisk the cream to a semi-whipped consistency (see page 16). Set it aside in the refrigerator.

Put the sugar (a) and 35 ml (1¼ fl oz) water in a small saucepan over medium heat and create a syrup by cooking until the temperature reaches 117°C (243°F). (If you don't have a sugar thermometer, use a teaspoon to take a small amount of the sugar syrup and drop it into a bowl of chilled water. If it is the correct temperature, the sugar will create a pliable ball when you pick it up.)

When the sugar syrup starts boiling, use an electric mixer with a whisk attachment to beat the egg whites and cream of tartar on low speed until medium peaks have formed. When the sugar syrup reaches the correct temperature, pour it directly into the egg whites, still whisking, to make an Italian meringue. (Try to ensure the boiled syrup doesn't hit the whisk.) Continue whisking the meringue until it cools slightly and then remove it from the mixer and set aside.

In a clean bowl using the electric mixer with a whisk attachment, beat the egg yolks and sugar (b) on high speed until light and aerated. Melt the chocolate in a double boiler or in a plastic bowl in the microwave (see page 12). Fold the melted chocolate into the meringue with a spatula, then fold through the egg yolk mixture and finally the semi-whipped cream.

Transfer the parfait mixture to a piping (icing) bag with a 1 cm (½ inch) plain nozzle (or use a spoon), and fill the prepared paper cones. Immediately place the cones in the freezer for 3–4 hours to set. This parfait can be made up to 3 weeks in advance if kept frozen, wrapped and stored in the freezer. 👉

1. *Roll the cut paper triangles.*

2. *Continue rolling to create a cone shape and fold in the end to secure.*

3. *Pipe the parfait into the paper cones and freeze.*

4. *Flick the sugar over two suspended oiled wooden handles.*

5. *Bunch the sugar threads together.*

6. *Wrap the sugar immediately around the parfait.*

STRAWBERRY SAUCE

250 g (9 oz/1⅔ cups) strawberries, hulled
200 g (7 oz) caster (superfine) sugar
½ teaspoon vanilla bean paste

Roughly dice or slice the strawberries and put them in a bowl that fits snugly over a medium saucepan. Cover with the caster sugar and add the vanilla bean paste. Half-fill the saucepan with water and put it over medium heat until it starts to simmer. Place the bowl of strawberries on top of the saucepan and simmer the strawberries for 3–4 hours, stirring regularly. Top up the water in the saucepan as needed. (The sugar will extract all the juice from the strawberries.) Leave the strawberries and juice together until required. This can be made up to 2 days in advance and stored in the refrigerator.

Just prior to serving, pass the mixture through a sieve, pressing with the back of a spoon to remove all the juice from the strawberries. Discard the strawberry pulp and keep the sauce aside ready for assembly. If not using straight away, the sauce can be stored in the refrigerator for up to 2 days.

SPUN SUGAR

300 g (10½ oz) caster (superfine) sugar
60 g (2¼ oz) liquid glucose

Put the sugar and 120 ml (4 fl oz) water in a saucepan over high heat and bring to the boil. Add the glucose and continue boiling until the temperature reaches 162°C (324°F). (If you don't have a sugar thermometer, focus on the colour of the bubbles on the surface of the caramel. As soon as the bubbles take on a light golden colour, remove the saucepan from the heat.) Have a bowl of iced water on hand and if the caramel starts going too dark after you have removed it from the heat, submerge the base of the saucepan into the iced water. Let the caramel sit at room temperature until the bubbles completely dissipate.

Spray two wooden spoon handles, or something similar, with vegetable oil and rub it into the surface. Cover the floor with old newspapers (or do this outside). Lie the two wooden handles on a work surface, approximately 30 cm (12 inches) apart, so that they are sticking out from the edge and hanging over the paper. Place two forks into the prepared caramel and use a flicking motion to create thin strands. Continue to flick until you have enough sugar to bunch together to make a sugar ribbon approximately 30 cm (12 inches) in length. You can fold it in half if necessary.

One at a time, take each parfait out of the freezer and unmould it, leaving the rest in the freezer. Wrap the sugar ribbon around the cone in a spiral fashion and cut off any additional ribbon with oiled scissors. The parfait can either be placed directly on a plate for serving or placed back in the freezer to store for up to 6 hours. Repeat the process until each parfait has a spun sugar ribbon. The spun sugar, when left at room temperature, will dissolve in between 20 minutes and 1 hour due to the moisture in the atmosphere. Freezing as soon as possible will ensure that the ribbon will stay intact. You can reheat the caramelised sugar over low heat as needed until it becomes liquid again.

ASSEMBLY

100 g (3½ oz/⅔ cup) strawberries, hulled and finely diced

Place a parfait with the spun sugar ribbon in the centre of each plate, trim the base if needed to ensure it sits flat. Drizzle strawberry sauce around the outside of the plate – this is sometimes best done at the table so the sauce doesn't run too much. Scatter the diced strawberries into the sauce and serve.

CHOCOLATE TRIFLE

SERVES: 12 DIFFICULTY: 🍫🍫 **GLUTEN-FREE**

I often have friendly competition at work with my colleague and friend Paul Kennedy. He holds the title of 'Trifle Master' which he's easily held for the last 10 years. I'm hoping that with this creation I can score some of my own trifle points. The trifle bowl I have used in this recipe holds 1.5 litres (52 fl oz/6 cups) of water.

FLOURLESS CHOCOLATE SPONGE

120 g (4¼ oz/about 6) egg yolks

70 g (2½ oz) caster (superfine) sugar (a)

150 g (5½ oz/about 6) egg whites

pinch of cream of tartar

75 g (2¾ oz/⅓ cup) caster (superfine) sugar (b)

25 g (1 oz) Dutch-process cocoa powder

60 g (2¼ oz/½ cup) cornflour (cornstarch)

80 g (2¾ oz) good-quality dark chocolate, coarsely chopped

Preheat the oven to 165°C (320°F) and line a 40 x 30 cm (16 x 12 inch) baking tray with a non-stick mat or baking paper. Using an electric mixer with a whisk attachment, beat the egg yolks and sugar (a) together on high speed until light and creamy. Remove from the mixer and set aside at room temperature. In a separate clean bowl, whisk the egg whites and cream of tartar on high speed until medium peaks form. Gradually add the sugar (b) and continue mixing for 1 minute to dissolve the sugar.

Sift the cocoa powder and cornflour onto a sheet of baking paper. Melt the chocolate in a double boiler or in a plastic bowl in the microwave (see page 12). Fold the sifted dry ingredients and melted chocolate through the whipped egg yolk mixture. Incorporate this mixture into the whisked egg whites by folding it in gently with a flexible spatula. Pour the mixture onto the baking tray, spreading it out evenly right to the edge, using a metal spatula. Bake for 12–14 minutes. To determine when it is baked, press gently on the surface and it should bounce back. Remove the sponge from the oven and leave on the tray to cool at room temperature. You can freeze the sponge at this point for up to 1 month.

Cut individual crescent shapes 4–5 cm (1½–2 inches) in size using an overturned glass or round cutter (first cut out a circle, then again to create a crescent shape) and keep the sponge wrapped in plastic wrap to avoid it drying out.

COCOA ARABESQUE

100 g (3½ oz) icing (confectioners') sugar, sifted

40 ml (1¼ fl oz/2 tablespoons) orange juice

40 g (1½ oz) unsalted butter, melted

30 g (1 oz/¼ cup) cornflour (cornstarch), sifted

10 g (⅜ oz) Dutch-process cocoa powder, sifted

Preheat the oven to 170°C (325°F) and line two baking trays with a non-stick mat or baking paper. Mix together the icing sugar, orange juice and the warm melted butter in a bowl using a spatula until combined. Add the cornflour and cocoa powder and combine without over-mixing. Spread the mixture out thinly over the trays using a palette knife. Bake for 10–12 minutes. Leave on the trays to cool at room temperature. Test a piece – once cool it should snap. If it is elastic or stretchy, simply put it back in the oven for a few minutes to cook further. When cool, store in an airtight container until required. This can be stored for up to 3 days. If it becomes soft, crisp it up again in the oven for a few minutes.

CHANTILLY CREAM

280 ml (9½ fl oz) cream (35% fat)
125 g (4½ oz) caster (superfine) sugar
½ teaspoon vanilla bean paste

Put the cream, sugar and vanilla bean paste in a mixing bowl and whisk until the cream just holds its shape but still collapses. Store the cream in the refrigerator for up to 1 hour before assembling the trifle.

CHOCOLATE GARNISH

150 g (5½ oz) good-quality dark chocolate

Temper the chocolate (see pages 12–14). Place the chocolate in a paper piping (icing) cone (see page 19) and cut a small amount off the tip of the cone with scissors and pipe or teaspoon a dollop at a time onto a sheet of baking paper. Using the base of a teaspoon, swipe in a curve from the centre of the chocolate outwards. Leave the decorations at room temperature for 30 minutes to set. If your room temperature is above 22°C (72°F), place the decorations in the refrigerator for no more than 5 minutes. The chocolate garnishes can be made in advance and stored below 22°C (72°F) for up to 2 weeks.

MILK CHOCOLATE MOUSSE

320 ml (11 fl oz) cream (35% fat) (a)
245 g (8½ oz) good-quality milk chocolate, finely chopped
40 g (1½ oz/about 2) egg yolks
15 g (½ oz) caster (superfine) sugar
85 ml (2¾ fl oz) milk
85 ml (2¾ fl oz) cream (35% fat) (b)

Whisk the cream (a) to a semi-whipped consistency (see page 16). Set it aside in the refrigerator. Put the chocolate in a medium heatproof bowl. Whisk the egg yolks and sugar together in a bowl by hand. Put the milk and cream (b) in a saucepan over medium heat and bring to the boil. Pour the hot cream over the egg yolk mixture and whisk to combine. Return the mixture to the pan over low heat, stirring gently with a spatula or wooden spoon, until the temperature reaches 82°C (180°F), to create an anglaise. (If you don't have a sugar thermometer, dip a wooden spoon in the mixture, lift it out and draw a line through the mixture on the spoon with your finger. If the anglaise runs straight over the line, it's not ready. If the line holds, it's ready. Do this quickly, before the anglaise runs off the spoon.)

Once the anglaise is ready, immediately strain it over the milk chocolate, whisking until the chocolate is melted. Fold through the semi-whipped cream with a flexible spatula. Use the mousse as soon as it is made.

ASSEMBLY

fresh raspberries, for garnishing

Start by placing one-third of the sponge crescents that will lock in together in the base of the trifle bowl with a layer of cocoa arabesque. Cover that with half of the chantilly cream and then half of the milk chocolate mousse. Add a layer of the remaining sponge crescents then another layer of cocoa arabesque, followed by the remaining chantilly cream and milk chocolate mousse. Place the trifle in the refrigerator for a minimum of 2 hours to set. It can be stored for up to 2 days. Just before serving, garnish the top by sticking the remaining broken pieces of cocoa arabesque and the chocolate garnishes into the milk chocolate mousse and then scatter fresh raspberries on top.

Chocolate Trifle PAGE 242

Chocolate Creamer Stack PAGE 246

CHOCOLATE CREAMER STACK

SERVES: 6   DIFFICULTY: 🍫🍫   **GLUTEN-FREE**

The elements in this dessert can all be pre-made and stored, and assembled on the day you're serving it. You can also replace the chocolate discs with chocolate meringue discs from the Concorde mousse cake (page 186) made in the same size.

CHOCOLATE CREAMER

170 g (6 oz) good-quality dark chocolate, coarsely chopped

60 g (2¼ oz/about 3) egg yolks

40 g (1½ oz) caster (superfine) sugar

280 ml (9½ fl oz) cream (35% fat)

Put the chocolate in a heatproof bowl. In another bowl, whisk the egg yolks and sugar together by hand. Put the cream in a saucepan over medium heat and bring to the boil. Pour the hot cream over the egg yolk and sugar mixture and whisk to combine. Return the mixture to the pan over low heat and stir constantly with a heatproof spatula or wooden spoon until the temperature reaches 80°C (176°F), to make an anglaise. (If you don't have a sugar thermometer, dip a wooden spoon in the mixture, lift it out and draw a line through the mixture on the spoon with your finger. If the anglaise runs straight over the line, it's not ready. If the line holds without any drips, it's ready. Do this process quickly, before the anglaise runs off the spoon.)

Once the anglaise reaches temperature, immediately remove the pan from the heat and strain the anglaise over the chocolate, whisking until the chocolate is melted. Transfer to a bowl, or preferably a rectangular container, and cover with plastic wrap directly on the surface of the creamer. Place in the refrigerator to set for approximately 1–1½ hours. The creamer can be made up to 3 days in advance.

VANILLA ANGLAISE SAUCE

55 g (2 oz/¼ cup) caster (superfine) sugar
60 g (2¼ oz/about 3) egg yolks
150 ml (5 fl oz) cream (35% fat)
75 ml (2½ fl oz) milk
1 vanilla bean, seeds scraped

Whisk the sugar and egg yolks together in a heatproof bowl by hand. Put the cream, milk and vanilla bean seeds in a saucepan over medium heat and bring to the boil. Pour the hot cream over the egg yolk mixture, whisking constantly to combine. Return the mixture to the pan over low heat, stirring gently with a heatproof flexible spatula or wooden spoon, until the temperature reaches 82°C (180°F), to create an anglaise. (If you don't have a sugar thermometer, dip a wooden spoon in the mixture, lift it out and draw a line through the mixture on the spoon with your finger. If the anglaise runs straight over the line, it's not ready. If the line holds without any drips, it's ready. Do this process quickly, before the anglaise runs off the spoon.)

Once the anglaise reaches temperature, immediately remove it from the heat and strain it into a bowl over an ice bath. Once it has started to cool, cover with plastic wrap directly on the surface of the anglaise and place it in the refrigerator until required. This can be made up to 3 days in advance.

CHOCOLATE DISCS

280 g (10 oz) good-quality milk chocolate, coarsely chopped

Temper the chocolate (see pages 12–14). Spread the tempered chocolate onto a sheet of acetate or baking paper in a thin layer with a palette knife. Just as the chocolate sets, using 8 cm (3¼ inch), 6 cm (2½ inch) and 4 cm (1½ inch) cutters, cut out six discs of each size. Leave the discs on a flat surface at room temperature for a minimum of 30 minutes to set. Alternatively, place the discs in the refrigerator for 10 minutes to set. The chocolate discs can be made up to 1 month in advance and stored below 22°C (72°F) in an airtight container.

ASSEMBLY

assorted fresh berries, for serving

To assemble the dessert, place a small dot of chocolate creamer on each serving plate and secure the largest chocolate disc. Warm a spoon in a bowl of hot water then scoop chocolate creamer onto each disc. Place the 6 cm (2½ inch) chocolate disc directly on top, on an angle. Follow this with another scoop of chocolate creamer and top with the smallest disc. Garnish the plates with berries and the vanilla anglaise sauce.

EQUIPMENT NOTES

Acetate: A firm plastic sheet that can be sourced from art stores or cake decorating stores. You can also use overhead projector transparency sheets but they will need to be cleaned before use. You can generally re-use acetate as long as you don't cut on it.

Bain-marie: A bain-marie is a hot water bath used to cook or melt ingredients slowly, away from direct heat. There are different types of bain-marie, but for the purposes of this book we mainly use a type also known as a double boiler. You can easily create a double boiler by half-filling a saucepan with water and bringing it to the boil over high heat. You'll need a heatproof bowl that fits snugly on top of the pan, to prevent steam from escaping. Once the water is boiling, either turn off or reduce the heat and place the heatproof bowl on top of the pan. Make sure the water in the pan does not touch the bottom of the bowl. Put your chocolate, or other ingredient, in the bowl to slowly melt.

Baking mat: A baking mat is a non-stick silicon surface that can be used in lieu of baking paper in some instances. It's a more economical option if you do a lot of baking as it's reusable – as long as you don't cut the surface. Ensure you keep the mat flat when storing it.

Baking paper: Also called parchment paper or silicone paper, baking paper is a treated non-stick paper used extensively in baking and pastry.

Cake ring: A cake ring is a metal ring without a base, used to create baked cakes and mousse cakes. As there's no base, there's no need to tip a cake upside-down to remove it from a cake ring.

Cake turntable: A cake turntable is a stable, rotating plate that enables you to decorate your cakes and other baked goods easily.

Chocolate mould: I use polycarbonate moulds as they are simple to work with, easily cleaned and give a great glossy finish to chocolate. You can also use plastic chocolate moulds. Both types can be sourced from cake decorating suppliers and some craft stores.

Dipping fork: A specially designed fork with two to four thin metal prongs designed for dipping chocolate.

Paddle attachment: This is an attachment for an electric mixer that is used to create doughs and pastry without creating too much aeration.

Paper piping (icing) cone: Individual triangles cut from baking paper approximately 32 x 24 x 23 cm (12¾ x 9½ x 9 inches) rolled into a cone shape ensuring the tip is closed. The ends of the paper are folded into the cone to secure it.

Piping (icing) bag: You can purchase cloth or disposable piping bags. You can also create your own paper piping cone (page 19), or zip-lock bags with a bottom corner snipped off can also come in handy.

Spatula: I use heat-proof silicon flexible spatula for most of my cooking. If you're a keen cook I recommend that you invest in a couple.

Tart ring: Like a cake ring, this is low metal ring without a base used for cooking tarts. You always get a better result when you bake a tart without a metal base and it makes them easier to handle. You'll find tart rings in specialty cookware stores.

INDEX

Page numbers in *italics* refer to photographs.

ACKNOWLEDGEMENTS

This book would not be possible without the amazing support I received. I would like to thank the following people for believing in me and for all their help and assistance:

Thanks to my husband, Michael, for your moral support and precious love. You seem to agree with everything I suggest and that gives me the confidence to achieve miracles. My son, Charlie – you are my biggest fan and chief taste tester – thank you for your thoughtful insight on all of my creations. Mum, thanks for all the support and for looking after Charlie when I needed to make cakes. Dad, wish you were here to see this book. Paul Kennedy, you spark my passion and are an endless source of inspiration – you do wonderful things for Savour. Gary Willis, my chocolate dealer, of whom nothing is too much to ask. Your belief in me is appreciated.

Thank you to the team at Murdoch Books: Sue Hines for understanding my vision of creating this chocolate book and allowing me to achieve it. Corinne Roberts, my publisher – your feedback, enthusiasm and insights were greatly valued. Katie Bosher for your editorial work and Paul McNally for editing the book. Hugh Ford and Aileen Lord for your design work. Greg Elms for your sensational photography and Georgia Young for your styling.

Special thanks to Jean Kirkland for your dedication and hard work on all my projects, in particular this book. Bee Tiew, Robyn Curnow and Janine Sang for all your help with recipe testing. To the Savour team for their work on the book: Stacey Alfred for helping with the edit, Damien Bilyk for your clever multimedia skills and input, Jessica Saikali, Kim Masciotra, Pat Pollard, Belinda Blazely, Victoria Bishop, Santiago Cuyugan and Jaimie Hunt.

Thanks to Karen Main-Krzysik, Jacquie Whitelaw and Jane Carbone, for testing these recipes out in your homes. Thanks to Peter and Janet Louros for keeping Charlie entertained while I made biscuits.

Robbie Mayer and Sam Mayer from F. Mayer Imports, your unconditional support is really appreciated. Thanks to Kay Cadman and Cedar Hospitality for your beautiful plates and props. And a big kiss to Filiz Bensan.

Finally, thank you to the following companies for the amazing products they produce and for the inspiration they provide for my work: Callebaut chocolate, Heilala Vanilla, Bulla Family Dairy and Unox.

The *MasterChef* judges call her 'the queen of chocolate', and Kirsten Tibballs has certainly built a formidable reputation as one of Australia's most celebrated and internationally respected pastry chefs and chocolatiers. When she is not teaching classes at Melbourne's Savour Chocolate and Patisserie School, which she founded in 2002, Kirsten travels the world, teaching classes, doing demonstrations and representing her country in competitions. Her handmade chocolates have won 'best in the world' at the World Pastry Championships in Las Vegas, and she has taken home a gold medal from the Pastry Olympics in Germany. Kirsten has been a judge at the World Chocolate Masters in Paris, the Patisserie Grand Prix in Japan and the World Chocolate Masters National selections in London. Her greatest passion is creating and sharing her recipes and techniques.

Published in 2016 by Murdoch Books, an imprint of Allen & Unwin

Murdoch Books Australia
83 Alexander Street
Crows Nest NSW 2065
Phone: +61 (0) 2 8425 0100
Fax: +61 (0) 2 9906 2218
murdochbooks.com.au
info@murdochbooks.com.au

Murdoch Books UK
Ormond House
26–27 Boswell Street
London WC1N 3JZ
Phone: +44 (0) 20 8785 5995
murdochbooks.co.uk
info@murdochbooks.co.uk

For Corporate Orders & Custom Publishing, contact our Business Development Team at salesenquiries@murdochbooks.com.au

Publisher: Corinne Roberts
Editorial Manager: Katie Bosher
Design Managers: Hugh Ford & Emily O'Neill
Project Editor: Paul McNally
Designer: Aileen Lord
Photographer: Greg Elms
Stylist: Georgia Young
Recipe Development: Kirsten Tibballs
Production Manager: Alexandra Gonzalez

ISBN 978 1 74336 612 7 Australia
ISBN 978 1 74336 613 4 UK

A catalogue record for this book is available from the British Library.

Colour reproduction by Splitting Image Colour Studio Pty Ltd, Clayton, Victoria
Printed by 1010 Printing International Limited, China

IMPORTANT: Those who might be at risk from the effects of salmonella poisoning (the elderly, pregnant women, young children and those suffering from immune deficiency diseases) should consult their doctor with any concerns about eating raw eggs.

OVEN GUIDE: You may find cooking times vary depending on the oven you are using. The recipes in this book use fan-forced ovens. For a standard oven, as a general rule, set the oven temperature 20°C (35°F) higher than indicated in the recipe.

MEASURES GUIDE: We have used 20 ml (4 teaspoon) tablespoon measures. If you are using a 15 ml (3 teaspoon) tablespoon add an extra teaspoon of the ingredient for each tablespoon specified.